FROM
VICTIM
TO
VICTORY

Other Books by Phil Quinn

Cry Out! Inside the Terrifying World of an Abused Child

Renegade Saint: A Story of Hope by a Child Abuse Survivor

The Well-Adjusted Child:
  How to Nurture the Emotional Health of Your Children

Spare the Rod: Breaking the Cycle of Child Abuse

The Golden Rule of Parenting: Using Discipline Wisely

FROM
VICTIM
TO
VICTORY

Prescriptions from a Child Abuse Survivor

Phil E. Quinn

Abingdon Press
Nashville

FROM VICTIM TO VICTORY:
PRESCRIPTIONS FROM A CHILD ABUSE SURVIVOR

Copyright © 1994 by Phil E. Quinn

This book is printed on recycled, acid-free paper.

Information in Appendix 2 is adapted from Michael J. Scott and Stephen G. Stradling, *Counseling for Post-Traumatic Stress Disorder* (Newbury Park, Calif.: Sage Publications, 1992).

Library of Congress Catalog Card Number: 94-79240

ISBN 0-687-13655-5

94 95 96 97 98 99 00 01 02 03 04 — 10 9 8 7 6 5 4 3 2 1

MANUFACTURED IN THE UNITED STATES OF AMERICA

To my wife,
Nancy,
in whose love and acceptance
I have recovered much,
and to all others
who seek the truth about themselves

ACKNOWLEDGMENTS

There is a line from a wonderful, old hymn that reads, "I was blind, but now I see." Much of my life has been spent in darkness with only the light of my hope to guide me. If left alone with my defective sight, I would be there still. But there are those in my life who occasionally allow me to "borrow their eyes" to see when my own fail me. Without their vision, their ability to see beyond the ordinary, this book would not be. I want to thank Beth Nash for taking her precious time to read the manuscript with the eyes of youth and of a public servant, and offer me such warm support. I am deeply grateful to her mother, Gayle Nash, not only for her valuable suggestions for improving the manuscript, but for the kind and gentle spirit of her friendship and for allowing me a small place in her world. To the Reverend Bill and Carol Dalglish, once again I thank you for being there for me. Dear friends for many years, your belief in me and continued support lifts me to new heights where I can see like an eagle! You pushed me gently to a new awareness and new insights. This book is richer for your gift to it! Finally, to my wife, Nancy, I extend my greatest thanks. Unfailing in her support, untiring in her reading and editing, unselfish in her sharing of my time, this book is as much an expression of her heart as it is of my hand.

CONTENTS

INTRODUCTION   11

Chapter One   Seeing Is Believing   **19**

Chapter Two   The Vital Balance   **27**

Chapter Three   Survival Behavior   **41**

Chapter Four   Why We Behave the Way We Do   **53**

Chapter Five   The Damaging Effects of Abuse   **71**

Chapter Six   Addictions   **93**

Chapter Seven   Posttraumatic Stress Disorder
                in Victims of Child Abuse   **105**

Chapter Eight   Finding Relief for Symptoms   **119**

CONCLUSION   143

APPENDIX 1   147

APPENDIX 2   149

APPENDIX 3   155

APPENDIX 4   159

NOTES   163

INTRODUCTION

Most civilized societies acknowledge a need for the state to provide a police force to protect family members from those outside the family who would do them harm. Witness the massive police force present in our own country. But it has only been recently, over the past several decades, that we have recognized a need for the state to provide protection for family members *from other family members!*

That family violence is more common than stranger violence has been a painful and much resisted acknowledgment in the hearts and minds of a nation that prides itself on family life. The family is sacred, we believe, the building block of society. We want to believe that parents can and must be trusted to do what is in the best interest of children. We are told that the integrity of families and the authority of parents must be respected if we are to save the family.

The strength of a nation can be measured in the health of its families. And the health of the family can be seen in the condition of its children. It is clear that the family must be preserved if our culture is to survive. A sustained national effort to preserve the family is needed, *but not at the expense of its members!* How to strengthen the family while protecting its members is one of the most vital social issues facing us today. State involvement in family life trying to protect the weakest among us—our children—continues to be a hotly debated and contested community issue.

It is even more heartbreaking to realize that our cherished notions of "The Family" as a safe place, a sanctuary of peace and harmony, are not always true. Research and empirical evidence have shown that the home is not always a place of care, nurture, and protection for children. Instincts and good intentions are not enough to guarantee effective parenting. Not all parents have the knowledge, skills, patience, empathy, and compassion necessary to ensure safe and prosperous childhoods. The reality is that some parents will not protect their children from intentional harm. Nor will all parents do what is truly in the best interest of their children's health and welfare, as we once imagined. There are parents who don't know what is best for the growth and development of healthy, well-adjusted children. Many adults parent out of simple necessity with little if any preparation, more out of ignorance than enlightenment. Most of us do "situational" or "crisis" parenting rather than "planned parenting," that is, having a plan for how to effectively achieve our desired goals with our children. Most childhood and parenting hazards can be avoided through careful planning and preparation.

The harsh and brutal reality is that the home is one of the most dangerous places in society. Children are at highest risk of being starved, raped, assaulted, and murdered in the privacy of their own homes than anywhere else. Clearly and painfully, the home is not always a sanctuary of peace for many children, but instead, can be a prison of horrors—a place of pain, suffering, and sometimes death. Hundreds of children die every year from abuse and neglect. Thousands more are harmed and permanently affected by abusive childhood experiences. But it does not have to be this way! I believe that 80 percent of family violence and child abuse is preventable. No greater challenge faces our nation than the protection of our children. How well our nation survives depends upon how our children fare in childhood, for children live what they learn.

National attention began earnestly focusing on the problem of child abuse in the United States in 1974 when the 93rd Congress passed "The Model Child Abuse Prevention Act." A National Center for the Prevention of Child Abuse was established in Washington, D.C. A child protective service was organized, and model legislation proposed making child abuse a crime. Since then, much time, effort, and money have been invested to develop intervention programs designed to help victims recover from childhood abuse and, what is more important, prevent it from occurring in the first place.

Still gripped and muted by my own painful memories of an

abusive childhood, I was not able to speak out for victims of child abuse until early 1980. One day a civic leader naively invited me to speak about child abuse at a service club luncheon.

"We're hearing a lot about this child abuse business," he explained over the phone. "Why don't you come and tell us over lunch what you know about child abuse?"

With that auspicious invitation, I began my public life as a child advocate and crusader for healthy children living in safe families. I have been active in the child abuse prevention movement in this country ever since. I have spoken at national and state conferences, tried to raise interest through public awareness programs, encouraged personal involvement through educational events, and addressed issues of abuse and child exploitation through the media.

Some of you first met me as "Peter" in the book, *Cry Out! Inside the Terrifying World of an Abused Child* (Abingdon Press, 1984). Though painful to read, you learned of the severe abuse I experienced as a child and how I managed to survive childhood. You also learned that I am just one of the thousands who have had similarly abusive childhood experiences. There are thousands every year who suffer for being a child. The book is detailed and graphic, a real-life look at the horrors of child abuse. It continues to be widely used by clinicians, schools, and special interest groups as a primer for those wanting to gain a deeper understanding of child abuse, especially from the victim's perspective.

Prompted by your desire to know more, a sequel to *Cry Out!* was published. *Renegade Saint: A Story of Hope by a Child Abuse Survivor* (Abingdon Press, 1985) continues Peter's story beyond the years of abuse into adolescence and young adulthood, highlighting many of the effects and consequences of the abuse on his adult life. Its message is clear: though damaging, being victimized as a child does not preclude a happy, fulfilled, and meaningful life as an adult. Offering hope to other victims, *Renegade Saint* recognizes that recovery is usually a lifelong process, often involving uncomfortable periods of adjustment and readjustment. In most cases, the prognosis for recovery from hurtful childhoods is good for those who pursue it diligently and faithfully.

Many of you have questioned why these books were written in third person—like novels—and why the name "Peter" was used instead of my own. That was not by accident.

1. Victims of abuse, particularly children, often find it easier and

safer to describe what's happening to someone else than what has happened to them. By projecting my experiences onto Peter, I could discuss the abuse in detail without fearing the inherent dangers of self-disclosure (such as disbelief, rejection, ridicule, reprisal, etc.). These are common fears that inhibit victims from disclosing the abuse experienced in childhood.

2. Although the books detail my specific experiences as a severely abused child—because they are the ones I know best—they generally describe the experiences of many severely abused children. By crying out my own pain through Peter in the book, it is my hope to speak out for all suffering children everywhere who need protection from those who would do them harm.

3. You have noticed that Peter has no physical description in *Cry Out!* That's not by accident, either. Peter could be male or female, black or white, young or old. Peter could be *the abused child within you or the abused child before you!* The purpose for writing those books was not to attract attention to myself, but to draw attention to those helpless, hurting children all around us, in every community, who desperately need our help. Though a real person, "Peter" represents the abused child, whoever he or she may be.

The books have served their purpose well. Joining in a chorus of appeals from survivors and child advocates across the country, and heard as far away as Capitol Hill, the past decade has brought tremendous national attention to the plight of abused children in this country and abroad. Hardly a day goes by when terrible, often grisly, accounts of abused, maimed, raped, or murdered children do not appear in the nation's newspapers. Even more important, every day thousands of people go to work with one primary purpose in mind: to make families a safer place for children.

In other books (*Spare the Rod: The Golden Rule of Parenting*), and in my lectures, I have continued to advocate on behalf of children across the country. I have answered thousands of letters and phone calls from victims, as well as those who work with them to stop and prevent child abuse. In my travels I have learned much from the thousands of survivors I have met over the years. Now, more than ever, I believe that our best hope of preventing child abuse lies in five primary areas:

1. **Sex Education:** teaching sexual abstinence and self-control while providing effective contraception so that unwanted, inopportune pregnancies can be avoided. Children who just "happen" are

at higher risk for abuse and neglect than those children conceived out of purpose and love. Strengthening and streamlining the adoption system can help provide homes for unwanted children at high risk for abuse or neglect.

2. **Mandatory Parenting Education:** a minimal knowledge of child development, acquisition of basic parenting skills, with an emphasis on communication and problem solving, and an awareness of how child abuse can occur in families, early warning signals, and what to do early in the cycle to prevent it, should be a prerequisite for a marriage license or for taking the baby home from the hospital. A short course on "Family Violence and Child Abuse," the cycle of abuse, should be a part of mandatory premarital counseling. Preparation for parenthood curriculum at the high school level involving the evaluation of one's own upbringing could help prevent child abuse by identifying early problem areas and teaching alternatives. It is not enough to teach people how to make a living; we must also teach them how to live together in peace. Also, a short course on "The Emotional Effects of Divorce on Children" should be a prerequisite for being granted a divorce.

3. **Early Intervention Programs:** prenatal parenting education and postnatal early intervention programs involving home visits and well-baby checkups. Providing families with tangible support services (employment, child care, problem solving, and life maintenance) early and regularly, along with counseling and education, can help relieve many social conditions that contribute to the onset of abuse in families.

4. **Recovery Programs for Victims:** Clearly, one of the most high-risk groups for becoming abusive toward children are those who were abused themselves as children. For many, it is all they know. It is difficult for parents to feel the pain of their children when they are so overwhelmed by their own pain. In addition, raising children is a skill learned most often by watching our parents raise us. Abusive parents teach an abusive parenting style that will likely be repeated in the next generation unless a conscious effort is made to do things differently. It is important to recovery that childhood abuse be redefined in light of adult experience and opportunities. It is also important that victims who are physically adults but remain children emotionally be provided opportunities to emotionally grow up and beyond their victimization.

5. **Eliminating Corporal Punishment:** Using physical and verbal

15

violence to control children only breeds anger, resentment, and hostility, and creates a climate for more violence. In the minds of some, corporal punishment opens the door to sexual exploitation. The root of sexual abuse is the right and duty to violate a person's body violently—*for a person's own good!* The most common rationalization for physically abusing children is "discipline." It is called "righteous violence"—violence done to a child for the child's own good. One of the most common rationalizations for sexually abusing children is "sex education." It is called "righteous sex"—sex done to a child for the child's own good. The one inflicts pain and is supposed to make the child feel bad, while the other stimulates pleasure and is supposed to make the child feel good. In the distorted minds of some offenders, pain and pleasure are flip sides of the same coin. The "right" to inflict pain upon children brings with it the "privilege" of offering to make them feel good through sexual pleasure. The ultimate disrespect is to violate a person's body violently or sexually, regardless of age. *We cannot protect our children from sexual abuse until we first protect them from physical assault!* Children can be protected from physical and sexual assault only when we teach—and practice—a wholesome respect for human minds, bodies, and sexuality.

From Victim to Victory is a sequel to *Cry Out!* and *Renegade Saint.* It completes the trilogy: from victim to survivor to victor. It has been said that the best revenge is to survive. That may be true, but the best outcome for our lives is to *thrive in spite of the abuse—to live life victoriously!*

In *Cry Out!* I described the pain of abuse. In *Renegade Saint* I discussed the effects of that pain on a developing adolescent and young adult. Now, in *From Victim to Victory,* my goal is to help relieve the pain, to find ways to reclaim the rest of our lives through healing and recovery. Healing begins by acknowledging and treating our wounds. But recovery occurs only to the extent that we overcome the "congenital despair" aggravated by the abuse and restore our "congenital hope" for a good life. The most vital activity of recovery involves first identifying the distorted, faulty beliefs taught us by the abuse that now interfere with our growth, development, and adjustment. People tend to behave in ways consistent with their value/belief system. Then, through the process of "psycho surgery" involving "cognitive transplants," we must reprogram our knowledge database with facts and beliefs that more accurately reflect the truth about ourselves, others, and life.

While others controlled our lives as children, we can—and must—take control of our adult lives. The quality and content of the rest of our lives will depend on what we do and say today. We must assume responsibility for ourselves and the rest of our lives. This means that we must stop doing what hurts us, and start and continue doing what helps us.

In the pages that follow, I will share with you what I have learned the past decade about healing and recovery from child abuse. Though each of us is different and our experiences may not be identical, there are certain dynamics of healing that remain the same for all persons who suffer for having once been a child. Perhaps by reflecting on the path of my own ongoing recovery, you will better see the path of your own or that of someone important to you.

There is healing in sharing life experiences along the path of recovery. Just as important, there is hope in healing.

Nowhere is it written into law that victims of childhood abuse must be unhappy, miserable, alone, and poorly adjusted for the rest of our lives! *We do not have to suffer forever in a private prison of painful and frightening memories called "childhood"!* With each new day comes an opportunity to live life fully and victoriously. But we must be willing to *tempus praeteritum resolve et carpe diem*—that is, "release the past and seize the moment." When we find ourselves inspired and motivated more by what's going to happen today and tomorrow than by what happened yesterday, then we will truly know what it means to do more than just survive—to live life victoriously!

Phil E. Quinn
Nashville, Tennessee

CHAPTER

ONE

Seeing Is Believing

Beauty and ugliness exist simultaneously in all things. This simple truth is often overlooked by discriminating adults, but rarely lost on young children. They have the wonderful ability to look beyond the obvious, to see beauty in its radiant simplicity in ordinary places. This is because small children don't make judgments about what they see. They tend to value things simply because they exist. Can this be what Jesus meant when he said that we must become like children in order to enter the Kingdom? It isn't until they're older that adults teach them the skill of discrimination, that is, the ability to make judgments about people and things, to choose what is good and reject what is bad.

Unfortunately, not all judgments are accurate—especially those we make about ourselves and others. Making accurate judgments is an "ability" developed in childhood and will enhance our lives. It requires education, truth, and commitment. Making inaccurate judgments is an "inability" also developed in childhood and can diminish our lives. Its result is often a handicapping prejudice rooted in ignorance, deceit, and convenience. Abused children often suffer from an inability to make accurate judgments. It's common for them to misjudge themselves and others.

People usually appreciate beauty. It's an attractive quality that's valued because it makes us feel good. What's valued is admired and usually held in high esteem. People tend to protect, preserve, and possess what they treasure most.

Spring came early to my Middle Tennessee home this year.

FROM VICTIM TO VICTORY

Shortly after the first thaw, my youngest daughter Chelsea came racing into the house bubbling with excitement. Clutched in her small hands was a bouquet of dandelions.

"Here, these flowers are for you!" she announced proudly as she thrust them toward me, smiling with satisfaction. "Aren't they beautiful?"

Though I accepted her token of affection with thanks, I didn't value her gift as highly as did she. Where she saw *flower* I saw *weed*. Where she saw something beautiful that brought pleasure, I saw something ugly that would ruin my lawn if not controlled. Where her instinct was to preserve them in a bouquet, my reaction was to destroy them in a compost pile.

How could our perception of the same thing be so different, I wondered? Was it because of our age difference or the fact that I knew so much more about flowers? Or that my experience with flowers gave me a deeper appreciation of what constitutes floral beauty?

I don't think so to any of these questions.

My daughter saw a beautiful flower in the dandelion *because that's what she was looking for!* Oblivious to my judgments about dandelions, she saw its intricate design and rich color, and innocently celebrated its beauty as a heartwarming sign of life renewal in the aftermath of a bleak and weary winter. She was looking for spring and in the dandelion found it!

It's been said that beauty is in the eye of the beholder. Is this true? Does beauty exist only when it's perceived? Can the same be said for truth? Or God? I don't think so. God, truth, and beauty all exist whether we acknowledge them or not. Just as we can't deny God, only ourselves a relationship with God, so too we can't deny beauty, only our perception of it. It's the spiritually mature, those whose eyes, ears, hearts, and minds are open to truth who can look beyond the distractions of prejudice to see beauty where it truly exists—in all persons and things.

From earliest childhood we're taught to see what we want in ourselves, others, and the world around us. If we're looking for beauty, we'll find it. If we're looking for strength and goodness, we'll find those also. But if, instead, we're looking for what's ugly, weak, and bad, we'll find them for they, too, exist in all persons and things. All it takes is a quick look in a mirror to see what's wrong with us. But what's exciting is that this same mirror can also show us what's right with us!

What we see will affect how we feel about what we're looking at. My daughter wanted to preserve the dandelions in a bouquet because she saw beauty in them and they made her feel good. I wanted to be rid of them because they brought me no pleasure. I saw them as a blemish on the green expanse of my lawn. They brought back memories of endless hours in the hot sun weeding the yard. These are not pleasant memories that fill me with warm feelings about dandelions!

Every situation in life demands one of three basic responses from us: we can either avoid it, confront it, or accept it. The pleasures of life we gladly accept. Problems that inhibit our functioning and diminish our life satisfaction need to be confronted and resolved. But those things that threaten our lives, health, and welfare need to be avoided and escaped at all costs. Information derived from our senses of smell, touch, taste, sight, and hearing must be interpreted in light of what we already believe to be true so that we'll know what response is required of us in every situation. Our survival depends upon accurately interpreting and acting upon this information. It's the judgments we make that provoke our feelings, and it's these feelings that motivate us to act.

How we feel about what we're seeing will affect how we behave toward it. In the eyes of my daughter, the dandelions were a mysterious yet magnificent creation of nature, infinite in detail, their colors radiant and breathtaking. Cradled in her tender hands, they were priceless examples of the beauty that can be life. Her response was to protect, nurture, and preserve them in a bouquet for all the world to see.

My response to the dandelions, at first, was quite different. Weeds are pests that have no value. They're to be pulled out of the garden, not something important to be nurtured, watered, and fed! In contempt, I ignore them, step on them without a thought as I stroll through the yard, make every effort to be rid of them, and look forever beyond them to the beauty of others. My concern has been, it seems, for the flowers in the world, not its weeds.

Now months later, I'm struck by the ignorance of my reaction to the dandelions. According to *Webster's New Collegiate Dictionary* (1981), "contempt" means to hold in low regard, a lack of respect and reverence for something. How often, I wonder, do I look at the people around me and see some as "flowers" deserving respect and appreciation because they bring me pleasure, and others as "weeds" deserving nothing, for they bring me nothing but disdain. How much more I seem to value those who blossom in ways that I can appreciate and how quick I am to turn away from those who do not.

FROM VICTIM TO VICTORY

Isn't it true that every flower begins as a bud that must be nurtured if it's to bloom? Doesn't all human life deserve reverence as a gift of the Creator? Just as important, how often do I see myself as a weed in the garden of life, a blemish upon its vast beauty? And isn't that pitiful view a reflection of the way I was treated as a child?

I want to see people—and myself—as my daughter sees the first dandelions of spring. The process begins by opening my mind so my eyes can see the beauty in any flower—even a lowly dandelion. It continues by opening my heart so that my eyes can see the strength, goodness, and hope in the broken, bruised, and molested child that I was. It opens my spirit to God's loving acceptance so that my eyes can see that people are not valued by God for what they aren't, but for what they are! It concludes when I can see and accept myself, not as I was yesterday or might be tomorrow, but as I am today. Even in my brokenness, God makes me whole! Finally, through the innocent, accepting eyes of my daughter, I can see!

Children from abusive and dysfunctional families are taught to look for what's wrong with themselves, others, and the world around them. *This is one of the most damaging legacies of child abuse.* As victims, we're taught to see what's ugly, weak, and wrong with us, to ignore the good in us because it's the bad that makes us what we are and ever will be. It's the bad in us that people see and react to. It's the bad in us that separates us from them and seems to doom us to a life of misery and continued victimization. For most of us, seeing is believing.

Abused children are raised with a distorted view of reality; a perspective tainted by misinformation, deceptions, and lies. Trying to survive in a toxic and often hostile world, we develop beliefs that help us survive today, but which may threaten our survival tomorrow. It's ironic that the same adaptive behaviors that keep us safe as children by appeasing the abuser can jeopardize our lives later, as adults, by aggravating and alienating others. Survival in threatening environments often demands that we assume and expect the worst, always alert to danger, being constantly vigilant for those who would do us harm. We're confronted by our inadequacies and weaknesses, the focus always being, it seems, on what's wrong with us. We learn, for example, that survival demands that we trust no one, not even ourselves.

In my recovery I have learned that *it's as much a deceit to deny beauty where it exists as it is to deny ugly where it exists.* To speak only of what's wrong with me is to speak a half-truth. The other half of that truth is what's right with me. A major step in my recovery occurred when I began perceiving and accepting the truth—about myself, the world, and other people. The hope and possibility of overcoming my memories of victimization and of making a good life for myself grew in proportion, it seemed, to the extent that I was willing to accept the truth—the whole truth—about what happened to me and its impact on the rest of my life.

Like many victims, for years I brooded upon my abusive childhood experiences and its devastating effect on me. I grew up believing that it was the result of an incomprehensible madness that I could not control, but which I brought upon myself. After all, bad things happen to bad people, I believed. It occurred as a natural response to my innate badness, for which there is no cure, rendering me unlovable. Not worthy of love, I believed that I deserved the punishment, that my condition was hopeless, my life doomed, and that I was helpless to change any of it.

These were all faulty beliefs—lies and half-truths! Distortions of reality. Deceptions I learned from those I trusted to teach me the truth. Deceit all too often reinforced by an ignorant and careless society.

Half of the truth is that I was severely abused as a child. But the whole truth is that I survived childhood and now have an adult life I can live as I please. I'm free now to choose the ways of peace in all my relationships. I need not remain a victim. It's true that as a child I had no control over what was happening to me—that I was powerless. The whole truth is that today I have control of my life and how I live it. Its quality and content are up to me. It's true that I have many bad and frightening memories of childhood. The whole truth is that I have far more life memories today that bring me pleasure than bad memories that bring me pain. I have more reasons to celebrate my life than to regret it. It's true that I was physically crippled by the abuse. I'm legally blind in my left eye, have a partial hearing loss, and have scars that constantly remind me of the abuse. But the whole truth is that this doesn't mean that I can't see and hear; I just see and hear with a "limp." It's true that I was mentally crippled by the abuse. The whole truth is that this doesn't mean that I can't think; I just think with a "limp." It's true that I was emotionally and spiritually crippled by the abuse. The whole truth is that this doesn't mean that I can't feel and believe; I just feel and believe with a "limp." Recovery for me has been a process of recognizing and identifying my "limps," accepting them, integrating them into my self-concept, and then going on to live my life successfully in spite of them! *It's not the limps that cripple us, but the fear of being crippled!* It's the fear of trying and failing that keeps us from trying and winning. There are many examples of seriously impaired people who live successful, fulfilling lives in spite of their limitations!

Many survivors of child abuse have a dismal, fatalistic view of life: It's all chance and fate; it's being lucky enough to be in the right place at the right time or unlucky enough to be in the wrong place at the wrong time; life is what you do while you're waiting to die; life is "killing time" until time kills you. Because of our childhood "survival" orientation, people and life events are often perceived as threatening. What threatens survival must be avoided. So, with an attitude of distrust, we adopt an avoidance posture toward life and relationships. We control our vulnerability by avoiding the risk of betrayal through intimacy and the risk of failure through competition. To remain safe, we tend to sacrifice our hopes and dreams. We forfeit our life opportunities, too often seeing them as another chance to fail. The result is a life of self-denial and compromise: settling for what we can get rather than going after what we really want in life. We tend to settle for substitutes in our life: substitutes for intimacy, for self-confidence, fulfillment, and personal satisfaction. For too many of us, these substitutes involve intense transient experiences with people, events, and substances. Because they are intense, we often confuse them with intimacy and personal fulfillment. We misjudge their real meaning in our lives.

Too often victims of child abuse focus their attention on what they don't have, what they needed and didn't get, or what was taken from them in childhood that can't be returned. Such a deficit focus makes the emptiness deeper, the need more desperate, the memories more painful. Deficit thinking keeps us locked in a childhood prison of helplessness and despair. It keeps us hopelessly trapped in our faulty beliefs, captive to our ignorance, and in bondage to the will of others. Who among us would not feel poor and deprived if we constantly focus our attention on what "could" be ours but isn't, what others "ought" to do for us but don't, or upon what we "should" be but aren't? *Deficit thinking leads to deficit living!* Living out of emptiness is far less satisfying than living out of abundance. Abundant living occurs when we recognize the abundance in our lives, accept it with thanks, and then use it to benefit ourselves and others. What's exciting is that abundant life is available to all of us! Recovery begins when we change our perspective from fatalism to an opportunistic view of life. Life isn't a burden, a heavy responsibility to be avoided, but an opportunity to be seized at every moment! It's a chance to make things better.

Deficit thinking prevents recovery for victims of abuse and almost assures them of continued victimization. The key that unlocks that prison of despair is truth. The truth about yesterday, today, and tomorrow. The truth about all things. It's called reality. A life viewed, reviewed, and previewed through the lens of reality has hope; for even in its darkest moments, there is light. In hope there is the promise and possibility of a better tomorrow.

Truth requires that we focus as much of our attention on what we do have as on what we don't have. In recognizing and appreciating the abundance in our lives, we can keep our deficiencies in perspective. There's a measure of poverty in all wealth, because no one can "have it all" just as there is a measure of ignorance in all knowledge because no one can "know it all"! There will always be something lacking in our abundance. But in that abundance are the tools for recovery and a better life.

Recovery begins by accepting and embracing reality. A life built on reality can withstand the storms of life, remaining steadfast and secure in truth. But a life built around avoiding reality will likely suffer more in its retreat than if it had stood boldly to face life's challenges.

Recovery requires that I accept myself just as I am first before trying to become better. It means that I review my history and redefine it, view my present life situation and restructure it, and preview my future from an opportunistic perspective and claim it. It means that I find relief from the symptoms of distress that interfere with my functioning, find and replace my faulty beliefs, and then refocus my life around the truth—the whole truth. My life does not have to be controlled by the badness of others. Sometimes it takes the worst in others to bring out the best in us! In that truth I'll find freedom—the freedom that comes from being at peace with those things that I cannot change and taking charge of those things in my life that I can change. It's there, in that peace that passes all understanding, that I'll find my hope and possibility. *Accepting and fulfilling my possibility will move me from victim to victory!*

The Vital Balance

Life is born out of pain. The discomfort of bearing a child is a normal part of the birth process. Every new birth is preceded by a long labor, a labor of necessity, of course, and usually a labor of love as well. But giving birth can also be life-threatening to the mother. Inherent within that life-giving ritual is the most perfect love one person can offer another. Jesus identified the willingness to lay down one's life for another person as the greatest possible expression of love (John 15:13). Mothers must be willing to risk their health and well-being—and perhaps their lives—to give life to another. What greater expression of love for a child can there be? It's an unselfish risk and sacrifice most mothers make for their children without thought of consequence to themselves. Yet, like fathers, thousands of mothers every year abandon, neglect, and abuse their children. How can this be?

I thank my mother for giving me birth. God's gift of life came to me through her pain and sacrifice. Though I didn't grow up with her, I love her as much as I can love someone I don't know very well. Permanently separated from her at the age of five, it would be easy for me to be critical and regret what she didn't give me—the loving mother I needed most as a child growing up. But rather than remember her with regret, I choose to think of her with joy and thanksgiving for what she did give me—the opportunity to live a life of my own! My mother holds a place of honor and respect in my life, for without her I would not exist.

In her absence, God brought surrogate mothers into my life. I survived as a child, in part, because of the mothering I received from

27

my foster mothers, teachers, and counselors. My deprivation was lessened by their willingness to love me. Part of my recovery has been to recognize and accept their gift to me, and to offer them thanks.

Few events in life are as exciting as the birth of a child. It often sparks a celebration that brings families together in a liturgy of life renewal, a time of rebonding with fresh hope and commitment, a time of remembering the hopes and dreams of one's own life. People have children for many reasons. For some it's a desperate effort to "save" a failing marriage or to force a marriage commitment. For others it's an effort to find love in a child that is not received from others or an effort to relive one's childhood through the lives of children or to find fulfillment. At worst, it may be to collect more welfare money. At best, it's the joy and happiness that come with the birth of a child, which outweighs the pain of giving birth, that motivates people to continue having children. It's that same joy and the commitment it inspires that can motivate parents to nurture, provide for, and protect their children from harm.

As long as the pleasure of being a parent exceeds the pain of parenting, people tend to remain committed and dedicated to the task. But what happens when raising children becomes too overwhelming, too distressful and frustrating? When the pain of parenting exceeds its pleasure? When hopes and dreams of a happy life together are crushed under the weight of disappointment and disillusionment? When the harsh realities of life discourage even the most noble of parenting intentions? Parenting can then become an unrelenting burden, a joyless task of great inconvenience and distress. It's then that children are at highest risk of being abused or neglected. At best, parents abuse their children out of ignorance. At worst, the abuse can occur due to an impulsive drive to achieve a "quick fix" outlet for stress. The conscience is overridden or conveniently ignored, and the act occurs. Often perceived as the source of their distress, parents may seek relief from their suffering by attacking or neglecting the child. By attacking the child, they challenge and overcome their feelings of helplessness. Through acts of neglect or abandonment, they avoid these same feelings. Abusive parents try to regain control of their lives at the expense of the child. In either case, the child suffers.

Being born is to be given life—temporarily! Life is a tenuous and fragile state of being that cannot sustain itself for very long. Left alone without food and water, life will terminate itself naturally.

There are certain things that human beings must have on a regular basis if life is to be sustained. These are called "needs." Needs are those things required for survival.

Survival Needs

Survival requires that we take care of our bodies. Meeting our physical needs for food, water, oxygen, clothing, exercise, shelter, and protection is an important activity of everyday life. Deprive the body of material life necessities or assault the body so that its ability to function normally is compromised and the likely result is impairment or death. This is called physical assault and neglect, an all too common type of child abuse.[1]

Just as deprivation can threaten survival, so can excess. Too much food, water, clothing, or exercise can result in death as well. Physical illness can occur when the body is assaulted, invaded, deprived, neglected, or stressed beyond its ability to cope. Overeating, for example, can lead to obesity, a leading cause of heart attacks.

A healthy balance is required to sustain life while not depriving or overwhelming it. Physical health requires a balanced diet in all life necessities.

Physical child abuse and neglect typically threaten the body's ability to survive by depriving it of life necessities or by overwhelming its ability to heal and restore itself after inflicted trauma. What affects a child's body will also affect the child's thinking, feeling, and believing—every aspect of the developing personality. Overwhelming the regenerative and coping abilities of the body will provoke a survival crisis in the child: a crisis that will be resolved by an altered life or a lost life. The child will either adapt to the demands of survival at the moment or die.

Human beings also have mental lives with special needs: a need for information, education, training, stimulation, enlightenment, and understanding. We must also develop the ability to discern, evaluate, and make wise, sound choices, choices based more on fact than feeling, choices that will enhance our lives rather than diminish them. Without these needs being met, our survival may be put at risk out of ignorance, misinformation, and erroneous decision making. Our choices in life are limited when we don't know all the options. Poor choices are often made due to a lack of information or a perceived lack of options. At its earliest conception, more child abuse occurs from ignorance than intention.

FROM VICTIM TO VICTORY

Mental health is based on reality. To the extent we recognize, comprehend, and accept reality, we remain mentally healthy. Mental illness can occur when we try or are forced to avoid, deny, alter, distort, or extinguish reality. Mental abuse, the assault of, or erosion of reality is also an all too common type of child abuse. A healthy balance must be maintained between what we want to be true, what we think should be true, and what is actually true. Mental health requires that we be rooted in reality, branch out in truth, and blossom in honesty.

Mentally abusing children assaults or erodes their grasp of reality. It distorts their perception of what's real and what's not, what's true and what's not, as well as what's important and unimportant. Perceptions can be altered by external forces. Inaccurate perceptions can result in faulty judgments about ourselves, others, and the world around us. Behavior is a response to our judgment about a person or situation. Inaccurate judgments can lead to inappropriate behavior.

Mentally abused children live and function in an unbalanced world of half-truths and misinformation. Their world's imbalance will be in proportion to its misrepresentation of truth.

Human beings are more than just minds and bodies. We also have feelings and emotional selves. To be healthy we all need love, warmth, acceptance, security, achievement, approval, intimacy, and the ability to control our own destiny. Without these needs being met, we are likely to jeopardize our lives through fear and loneliness. The more desperate we become, the more irrational risks some of us are willing to take to make ourselves feel better. Desperate acts often have tragic consequences.

Emotional health is rooted in trust and acceptance of ourselves, others, and the world around us. It requires that we be in intimate community with other people and nature. It is through relationships that we achieve most of our happiness, satisfaction, fulfillment, and contentment in life. Emotional problems occur when we become alienated, estranged, abandoned, or disconnected in our relationships.

Emotional abuse, yet a third type of abuse, occurs when our ability to trust and accept ourselves, others, and the world is assaulted or eroded through neglect or deprivation. Emotional health requires that we remain vulnerable enough to trust and trust enough to stay connected to the people and places that make up the world of which we are a part.

Emotionally abused children live in the middle of an unending storm of conflicting thoughts and feelings. Our lives often become a sequence of impulsively acting out the turmoil within us as we attempt to calm the storm. Once again, judgment can be impaired by passion, often resulting in high risk or inappropriate behaviors—behaviors that threaten the health and welfare of ourselves or others.

Finally, there are our spiritual needs. All of us must have faith in something! It's our faith that allows us to face an uncertain tomorrow, day after day, with an attitude of hope and expectancy. We all must have hope for a better tomorrow, faith in a benevolent God and the goodness of others, belief in forgiveness and redemption for ourselves and others, and a certainty that God really is in control. There must be special meaning in life and for our presence in it. Without these important spiritual needs being met, we are likely to wither through apathy as we drift aimlessly on a sea of hopelessness and despair. Spiritual illness occurs when we begin to doubt the rationality, the goodness, the meaning, and purpose of life—seriously challenging the existence of anything beyond the limits of our own imagination. When God is experienced as aloof, distant, and remote, then God becomes impersonal and unknowable. Spiritual illness is doubting God. It's our doubting of God's presence, love, and forgiveness, more than our sin, that estranges us from God. We can remain in relationship with God, in spite of our sin, because God will forgive those who seek it with a penitent heart. But only we can bridge the chasm of doubt. Spiritual illness also can occur when we presume to know the mind of God in all things, for to fully comprehend God is to presume to be God. Imposed on a child, spiritual abuse is the distortion of God, the maligning and misrepresentation of God's nature. It is the refusal to allow children to come unto God.

Spiritual health requires a healthy balance of faith and reason: the one to understand our existence and the other to comprehend the existence of something greater than ourselves. People thrive in an atmosphere of respect for yesterday, expectancy for today, and hope for tomorrow. Combined with an abiding faith in a benevolent and loving God, life becomes a reverent act of personal devotion.

So long as the body can survive its age, life will flourish and sustain itself to the extent that these physical, mental, emotional, and spiritual needs are met. If all survival needs are met, it's not illness, disease, accidents, or inflicted injury that decide the length of our lives, but age. Then life terminates in old age.

Therapeutic Pain

Some people's perception of pain is that it's an abnormal condition, something to be avoided, escaped, or erased at all costs. The assumption is that pain—all pain—is bad for us. There's something "wrong" with a person who's hurting or in pain. If we can't relieve it with medication, then we try to minimize it through denial or anesthetize it through repression. We behave as though healthy people should never feel pain.

There are those who believe that God rewards the righteous with affluence, abundance, and freedom from suffering. Those who experience poverty, need, or pain are somehow being punished by God as though they deserve to suffer. So we must camouflage our pain in order to hide our shame.

This attitude has resulted in a manic effort by many people to pursue a state of "painlessness" similar to our pursuit of "agelessness." Millions of dollars are spent every year on nonprescription drugs so that we can self-medicate and ease our discomfort.

It's true that survival requires that we avoid too much pain. But it's also true that survival requires that we feel some pain some of the time. A complete state of painlessness is an unconscious state or death. Some pain is an early warning system to alert the mind that the body is at risk of serious harm. What would happen if we couldn't feel the pain of a hot stove or a deepening sunburn or a deep cut on a foot? Consider the pain of head and back aches, or hunger and fatigue, of loneliness, guilt, shame, and disappointment. Some pain motivates us to protect, feed, and nourish ourselves. Other pain motivates us to move, to act, to strive for achievement, relief, or reward. Every movement away from pain is toward relief.

Actually, something is wrong with a person who doesn't feel pain! From the moment we're born, pain is a natural part of the human experience. It's impossible to avoid it. We can only minimize and manage it.

Many survivors of child abuse believe they are "taking care" of themselves by avoiding the pain of their childhood abuse by ignoring, sedating, repressing, or denying it. It sometimes feels safer to not deal with the abuse. But this is illusion, an emotional mirage. The hurt and pain exist, whether or not we choose to acknowledge it. Our choice isn't whether or not to experience the pain, but instead, which pain will we experience. There's the pain that comes from cleansing and treating our wounds. This pain leads to healing and recovery. Or, there's the pain of leaving our wounds unattended, perhaps to fester and become infected. This pain only leads to more and deeper pain.

It's important for victims of child abuse to acknowledge, feel, and express their pain. There's relief in expression. Even more important, *there's healing in feeling.* We must confront our pain knowing that we have already survived the worst. If the abuse couldn't destroy or defeat us, then its memory can't either.

Victims can actually take the pain of their memories and use it to fuel an anger that can inspire them to act in positive, constructive ways to prevent the same abuse from happening to other children. It can be a powerful force in their recovery and in the protection of others.

This is what I've done in my own recovery. I've channeled the pain into anger. I'm angry about what was done to me as a child, but also because I know what happens to other children every day all over the world. This anger motivates me to stand in front of crowds to speak the truth about child abuse, to write books, to challenge parents to stop the hitting and initiate nonviolent problem-solving strategies in their families, and to continue advocating for the elimination of all violence—physical, emotional, sexual—in families. This anger gives me the strength to withstand the criticism and rebuke often encountered when I challenge families to change and "get well." It's my anger and the hope that comes from knowing I speak the truth compelling me to continue to lecture, to write, and to persist in my own recovery.

In my youth, my anger controlled me. It pushed me to hurt others as I was hurt. To control as I was controlled. To force my will on others as their wills were forced upon me. I thought there was power in getting even, of being able to do unto others before they do unto you. But I was wrong! In violence there is only weakness—and submission to a power greater than ourselves: rage! An important part of my recovery was learning to control my anger. As a victim, I expressed my anger with my fists, forcing people to see and hear me, to feel my pain through the pain I inflicted on them. In recovery, I have forsaken the ways of fists for the power of words. It's the same anger that drives me—just a different way of expressing it! Today, my anger serves me. It's my most important source of energy. It's my catalyst for change. In my pain, I have found healing.

Congenital Hope and Despair

Within all of us is an innate force that drives us to survive at all costs, an optimistic spirit that assures us sustaining life is possible so long as survival needs are met. Intrinsic within that optimistic outlook on life is the belief—the hope—that others, especially our parents, will take care of our survival needs until we are capable of taking care of them for ourselves. Even more important, it's our belief in a better tomorrow, that another day will follow night as another spring follows winter, that we will once again awaken in the morning to a new day in a new place with new opportunities. This I call "congenital hope." We are born with it. It is another of the Creator's gifts to us at birth.

Congenital hope sustains and enhances life. It inspires us to do more than merely survive. For in hope there are dreams, and in dreams, goals. Goals motivate us to act to improve the quality of life for ourselves and others. Achieved goals are the stepping-stones to a fulfilled and abundant life. Life unfolds within our aspirations. Its only limit is the limit of our hope. Congenital hope is maintained through an intrinsic faith in others—a faith that assures us people are benevolent, that they can be trusted not to hurt us and will give us what we need to survive. It's a belief that our parents will find us worthy, and so will accept and love us.

But for all things, there is an opposite. For macro, there is micro. For light, there is darkness. For good, there is bad. For up, there is down; for right, there is wrong. Even physics has acknowledged the duality of nature by describing the opposite of matter as antimatter. The opposite of proton is electron. The opposite of life is death.

Opposites define each other. They do so by telling us what the other is not. Ugly defines what beauty is not. Right defines wrong as night defines day. We cannot know one without at least suggesting the possibility of the other.

Opposites can also exist within each other. Light casts shadows, which is darkness. Darkness affects the brightness of light. A dim light, for example, contains more darkness than a bright light. The presence of "bad" affects the "goodness" of "good." What is the difference, for example, between a good person who serves others and a saint who serves others? Within all life is the presence of an approaching death. An atom exists because of the presence of both protons and electrons. To remove one or the other would be to destroy the atom. "Splitting the atom" refers to this very process during which there is a resulting burst of energy that could potentially destroy everything near it.

The opposite of congenital hope is congenital despair, that fatalistic force within all of us warning that we cannot survive outside our mother's womb. While in the womb, our life is sustained through the umbilical cord. As long as mother's life is sustained, our life will be sustained as well, unless, of course, it is naturally or therapeutically terminated. But life support to the child *flows naturally, without conscious thought or effort,* from mother to the child. After birth, when we become separated from mother, that natural flow of life support is cut off. Now we must rely on the conscious effort of mother and father to sustain life. Our congenital hope is that they will. But our congenital despair is that they will find us unworthy and will not.

Essential to congenital despair is the belief that others, especially our parents, will not love us enough to take care of our survival needs. We are afraid that they will reject and abandon us to survive alone in a malevolent world where there is little chance of survival without help. Whereas congenital hope inspires security and confidence, congenital despair provokes insecurity and fear within us. Congenital despair is rooted in fear and distrust, feelings of unworthiness and shame. With hope there is the possibility of a better tomorrow, while in despair there is only the certainty of a miserable ever after.

Congenital hope derives from the Creator's presence within us, that eternal breath of life breathed into us at birth which brings us immortality. It thrives in the knowledge that, in spite of our sin, God loves us so much that his son, Jesus, would be sent to die for us that we might live. Congenital despair, on the other hand, derives from our sinful nature, that mortal part of us that will do wrong in spite of our will to do right. It's the weakest part of us—most vulnerable to evil persuasion—that feels doomed and without hope. It thrives in an atmosphere of pessimism and self-doubt. Crippled by shame and guilt, we feel unlovable and so reject the Creator's gift that would be our salvation. Life seems hopeless.

Highest Hopes and Deepest Fears

Inherent within all sentient life are both congenital hope and its opposite, congenital despair. Congenital hope is an attitude of positive anticipation—seeking and anticipating the best with an expectation of fulfillment. Congenital despair, on the other hand, is an attitude of negative anticipation—seeking and expecting the worst—a sense of futility, helplessness, and resignation. Validating congenital hope brings feelings of pleasure, confidence, assurance, and peace. Validating congenital despair brings feelings of pain, fear, uncertainty, and unrest.

There are five primary forms of congenital hope and despair intrinsic to all human life:

1. **The Hope of Immortality; the Despair of Death.** It's impossible for human beings to imagine our own nonexistence. To ponder absolute nothingness is like pondering the vastness of the universe; it's beyond human comprehension. Beyond our faith in an afterlife, death is a mystery. For some it's a dark, menacing chasm of emptiness looming forever in the future, waiting to engulf us. For others it's a passageway to blessed relief from the pains and sorrows of mortal life. Once life begins, we assume by the way we live that it will never end. We expect that one day will follow another endlessly. We try to ignore the signs of advancing age that foretell an end to life as we know it. We cling tenaciously to youth in hopes of immortality.

Death can be a distressful and painful experience for the living because it forces us to contemplate the end of our own lives. In that contemplation we encounter our finiteness, our mortality, and ultimate helplessness. More specifically, we encounter our need for a savior, for there is nothing we can do to save ourselves.[2] In death, like never before, we come face to face with our absolute vulnerability and dependence upon God.

2. **The Hope of Control over Our Life; the Despair of Powerlessness.** Having the power to initiate change, to manipulate the environment, and to act on our own behalf to get what we want and need to sustain life is an important part of congenital hope. There's something frightening and defeating in the thought that we are

controlled by genetics, hormones, the environment, or the greater will of others around us. To be powerless is to be impotent and defenseless in one's life, desperately vulnerable and dependent upon the goodwill of others. Feeling helpless and unprotected forces us to imagine the worst that can happen to us.[3] Out of those imaginings arise our deepest fears. In these fearful imaginings we encounter our need for a comforter.

3. **The Hope of Intimate Fulfillment; the Despair of Loneliness.** Though physically separated from mother at birth, we retain a need to be connected to other people and the world around us. It's through relationships that our needs are met for intimacy, love, acceptance, companionship, comfort, and support. Part of what it means to be human is to be a social person, which requires interaction with others. To be estranged and separated from others is to be denied their warmth, love, and acceptance, all emotional needs for survival. Even more significant, to be ostracized negates our worth as a person, making us valueless to ourselves and often to others. That which is not valued need not exist. It's in our exile and aloneness that we encounter our need for a redeemer.[4]

4. **The Hope of Meaningfulness; the Despair of Worthlessness.** If life were but a random accident of nature, it would have no meaning beyond itself. To feel important enough to continue living, we must believe there's a reason for life, a purpose beyond our awareness perhaps, but a purpose for our lives nonetheless. We must have a status above the animals, a place of dignity and respect, so that our survival will be enhanced instead of threatened by others like us. In meaning there is worth. That which has worth has special meaning and that which means something special is worthy of acceptance. It's in our moments of meaninglessness and worthlessness that we encounter our need of a Lord who loves us enough to die for us.

5. **The Hope of Order; the Despair of Chaos.** Human life is organized around rationality; a series of laws and principles that govern how and why things exist and function as they do. There are the laws of physics, for example, and the laws of chemistry and medicine, the principles of a lawful society, the principles of mental and spiritual health. Life is rational and sensible, and follows a logical sequence. What's logical is comprehensible and predictable

to human beings. What's predictable is manageable and, therefore, controllable. In a world toxic to human life, being in control of oneself and the environment is critical to survival. Disorder and chaos are overwhelming because they imply a total loss of control. In rationality there is reason. And reason suggests intentionality in the mind of the Creator. Intentionality assures us that there is a master of the universe. The difference between sanity and madness is the difference between order and disorder. It's in our madness that we, more than at any other time, encounter our profound need of a Creator, a Lord and master in our lives who, despite our occasional doubts, truly is in control.

Our health and well-being as human beings depend upon how well we inspire our congenital hopes while overcoming our congenital despairs.

Any life experience that threatens our congenital hope or that aggravates our congenital despair will cause us distress. That distress will be expressed in us as physical, mental, emotional, and spiritual symptoms. The greater the threat, the greater the distress. The more intense the distress, the more dramatic the symptoms. Symptoms of illness exist to express our suffering. They warn us of impending difficulties and encourage us to take preventative and medicinal actions.

The Balance

Mental and emotional health requires a balance between our highest hopes and deepest despairs. We must maintain a reasonable faith in others as well as a reasonable fear of others; a balanced attitude that reflects the reality of life, ourselves, others, and the world around us. Mental and emotional health is rooted in reality: perceiving and understanding the world the way it really is, and then finding ways to live within that reality. Mental health is a balance between our unrealistic hopes and our unrealistic despairs. It's a balance between our faith and our doubt.

It's impossible to live without some pain in our lives. It's equally impossible to live without experiencing pleasure. A natural balance is a life that can cope and deal with pain—while minimizing it—and at the same time find, accept, and maximize pleasure. Mental health is affected by how well we are able to convert our unrealistic hopes and fears into more realistic ones. Emotional health is affected by how well we are able to resolve our fears and achieve our hopes.

When we are unrealistically hopeful or unrealistically despairing, we call ourselves "mentally unbalanced." Unrealistic hopes and fears can result in an imbalance that can cause enough tension and stress to result in neurotic mental disorders. But when unrealistic hopes and fears are severely aggravated by life experiences such as abuse and torture, enough distress can result in psychotic mental disorders. The goal of intervention and treatment is to help us regain that balance between our hope and despair, our confidence and our fear, our perception of truth and reality itself.

Mental health problems can occur when our confidence in ourselves, others, and the world becomes threatened, or when our fear becomes acute or aggravated.

Few experiences in life, with the exception of war and torture, can equal the threat to survival posed by child abuse. By its very nature, child abuse erodes the congenital hope of children while simultaneously aggravating their congenital despair. Because it is violent, dehumanizing, and so often painful, abuse brings children face to face with their own deaths, often long before they are capable of comprehending and coping with such a confrontation. It forces them to imagine and expect the worst, to detach themselves from others, to experience absolute powerlessness and vulnerability, and to mistrust the intentions and deeds of those upon whom they must depend for life. Child abuse denies, ignores, and thwarts the survival needs of children. By interrupting life support, life becomes fragile and tenuous. Too often, abused children must find a way to protect themselves alone and survive, or die. They are thrust prematurely into an adult world of power, violence, and sex, where reality becomes the will of the abuser. Submission and compliance is too often the price of survival.

A severe imbalance can occur that can leave the child teetering on the brink of self-destruction. Abused children are full of despair, their hope but a flicker in their doubts. Recovery requires that a balance be reachieved, that hope once again flame fiercely in the hearts of victims.

Survival Behavior

The most basic of all human instincts is to survive. Inherent within all of us is both the desire and the will to continue living. As human beings mature, we develop effective methods for coping with the endless stresses and challenges of living in a complex society. When confronted by an attacker, for example, we can run away, shout, hide, play possum, or cry.

As adults we have other tools available to us: the telephone, weapons, problem-solving strategies, automobiles, and counterattack.

Few people willingly surrender their lives without a struggle. When threatened, life takes on added value. Regardless of religious beliefs concerning the value of human life, most people will take a life in order to preserve their own.

This fundamental instinct to survive is reflected in the social and legal mores of our culture. The laws recognize that people have a right to survive, to protect themselves and their loved ones from harm. Self-defense is a morally, ethically, and legally justifiable reason for killing another human being in our culture. There is a growing awareness that parents not only have a right to survive, but also have a responsibility to ensure the survival of their children.

Children have a right to protect themselves as well. If parents do not assume responsibility for protecting their children, children will instinctively try to protect themselves. Their methods may be primitive and immature, but they may be the best the children can do. A major challenge for survivors of child abuse is how to make the transition from survival behavior, which focuses upon personal threat and deprivation, to thriving behavior, with its focus on personal freedom and opportunity.

The most extreme form of physical self-defense is to kill the attacker. This extinguishes the threat to our survival. The most extreme form of mental self-defense is to deny the existence of the attacker. We cannot be threatened by what does not exist. Ignoring the threat relieves us of painful, frightening, and perhaps overwhelming thoughts and feelings about the attacker that could impair our ability to survive. The most extreme forms of emotional self-defense is to avoid the attacker entirely or to surrender. Avoidance protects us from the intense feelings evoked in us by the attack. Surrender eliminates the need for continued assault. The most extreme form of spiritual self-defense is to forgive the attacker. This transforms the threat into a cry for help and the attacker into a person worthy of love, acceptance, and forgiveness. *Forgiveness is the antidote for evil.* It protects us by purifying our thoughts, strengthening our heart, and emptying our spirit of the poison that evil inflicts upon all it touches.

But what about children who don't have the knowledge, skills, or resources of an adult to protect themselves when under attack? How do children survive when trapped in the same house, perhaps the same room, with their attacker? Laws forbid children from running away from their families—even if their lives depend upon it! Crying helplessly may only infuriate the attacker more. Hiding from the attacker is impossible because there's no place to hide. Playing possum may only make the children more vulnerable to assault. Shouting at the attacker is sure to only intensify the attack. How can children survive when their every instinct is thwarted, when they are completely out of control and helpless to protect and defend themselves—when the abuser is so much bigger, smarter, and more powerful? This is the dilemma of every severely abused child.

Ordinary means of survival generally do not work in extraordinary situations of threat, such as severe child abuse. It takes extraordinary means in these extraordinary situations for children to survive physically, mentally, emotionally, and spiritually.

How We Respond to Life-threatening Situations

When threatened by our own death or the death of a loved one by violent assault, torture, accident, or natural disaster, every part of us—every sense—becomes focused upon finding a way to survive. Survival demands that we escape or overcome whatever is threatening us.

Survival often means staying in control and being able to act decisively on our own behalf. Anything that threatens the control we have over our lives potentially threatens our survival and must be resisted.

Human beings are a lot like the crew of the USS Starship *Enterprise* in the popular space adventure television series. When confronted by an unknown alien presence or force, the crew's first response is to "scan" the alien ship in an effort to learn more about it. The primary goal of the scan is to determine hostile or peaceful intent. This preliminary evaluation of the situation attempts to answer the question, Will the existence of the *Enterprise* and its crew be threatened or compromised by the alien, or will it be enhanced through peaceful contact with another life form? If there are no aggressive gestures by the alien ship, and the scan concludes that there are no weapons aimed at the starship, Captain Picard will likely conclude that it's safe to have contact with the alien ship. He will then become proactive toward the alien—that is, initiate contact. Communication channels will be opened and a communication link attempted. If these gestures of friendship are reciprocated, then the crew is likely to initiate more personal and sophisticated relationships with the alien beings.

Similarly, when we are confronted by a possible threat, our initial response is to "scan" the source of the perceived threat to learn as much about the intention toward us as possible. We listen intently, observe posture, facial gestures, eyes and hands, searching for some clue as to motivation. If we perceive that the intent is friendly, we will likely approach the person or allow him or her to approach us, in an attitude of cautious trust, acceptance, and a willingness to interrelate.

But what happens if the scan from all the sensing devices on board the *Enterprise* warns of hostile intent, identifying lethal capacities of the alien while observing aggressive maneuvering toward the starship? In this situation, rather than being proactive and initiating contact, Captain Picard's response is more likely to be reactive, a reaction of escape or avoidance, if possible. He will first go to "yellow alert," which puts all of the physical, mental, and emotional resources of the ship and crew on "standby readiness" in case they are needed to help escape or survive a possible attack. The primary goal of this alert status is to gather as much information in as short a time as possible—identify what they are confronting, ascertain the ultimate intent, assess the level of threat to the *Enterprise,* and prepare their defensive responses. Direct communication with the alien force may be attempted at this point by opening all communication channels and hailing the intruder in an effort to learn its intent directly. This heightened state of alertness is characterized by an increase in cardiovascular activity, such as respiration and heartbeat, an increase in physical and mental activity, a deeper level of concentration and a sharper focus upon the alien, and an increase in general nervousness and excitement in the crew.

Similarly, if our observation of the persons confronting us concludes that their intent is unfriendly, hostile, or dangerous, our likely response will be to avoid contact with them. We also will undergo the physiological changes of increased arousal caused by the additional stress.

Again like the *Enterprise,* if we perceive a threat and conclude that an attack is imminent and avoiding the conflict is impossible, then we will go to "red alert," during which we raise our defensive shields, go to full combat readiness, and then face our antagonist head-on, prepared to do whatever is necessary to survive the attack—even if it means attacking the attacker! Working feverishly behind our protective shields, we become fully engaged physically, mentally, emotionally, and spiritually in trying to find a way to either escape or overcome our attacker. If our initial efforts to defend ourselves fail, and our shields and defenses are breached, then we will retreat deeper and deeper into the ship, confining ourselves to only that part of the ship that we can defend, combining, intensifying, and refocusing all our resources in an effort to survive. As we become more desperate in our struggle to survive, our efforts to protect and save ourselves will become more desperate, involving more risks and acts of recklessness. If we are able to overcome our oppressor and gain victory, then we will reoccupy the ship and resume, in time, normal, routine functioning. But if our defenses are totally overwhelmed and defeat is imminent, then we will likely surrender control of the vessel as well as our lives to the intruder, believing that continued self-defense is futile and will fail. In defeat, we must resign ourselves to our fate, recognizing that we are now under the control of something or someone else. Being overwhelmed and overpowered by an intruder means that we must turn loose of the reality we have known and accept the reality imposed upon us—or die. Now we must believe, think, feel, behave as our conquerors require, because survival demands it. Truth and reality become subjective, a matter of personal perception in service of survival.

This is what it's like for children who are overwhelmed and abused by adults who are so much bigger, smarter, louder, tougher, and meaner than themselves—adults who have all the power, who can exert total control over the child. Survival becomes a process of regressive thinking, feeling, and behavior in search of survival—a process that becomes increasingly more primitive, adaptive, and desperate as the threat to survival becomes more serious.

Adaptive Defensive Behavior

When confronted by a threat that forces us to respond in a way that is out of the ordinary, there are four basic levels of adaptive responsive behavior: mature, crisis, neurotic, and psychotic defensive behaviors. Each of these levels of behavior is an attempt to reestablish control and a sense of well-being in one's life. Each level becomes more dramatic, intense, and desperate than the next, each being harder for other people to understand and accept.

1. Mature Defensive Behaviors. When confronted by a person or situation of minor, but uncomfortable, assault or deprivation, we are likely to respond to the threat using mature defensive behaviors. Our goal is to successfully resolve the issue or solve the problem with as little pain, conflict, and effort as possible while not making it worse. We seek relief from the uncomfortable feelings evoked in us by the problem. Some of the more common mature defensive strategies we employ include:

- *Vicarious Pleasure.* This involves seeking satisfaction in the pleasure of others. When unhappy parents have the power to inflict their unhappiness upon their children through words and fists, then it becomes important for the children to be able to find pleasure in pleasing their parents. Avoiding punishment through parental appeasement is an important survival tool.

- *Submission.* This involves placating the attackers, surrendering to their will and giving them what they want. During times of family distress, turmoil, and conflict, it is important that children submit to the will of their parents rather than force a confrontation. By meeting their demands, for example, there may be no need for the parent to attack.

- *Postponement of Gratification.* By setting aside their own wants and needs temporarily, children can avoid aggravating, irritating, or frustrating the parents or giving them reason to criticize or punish.

- *Minimization.* This involves not taking the situation too seriously. Children can seek to relieve the tension and cope with the anxiety of a distressful situation by minimizing its seriousness through the use of humor, play, rationalization, and selective forgetting.

- *Suppression.* This involves consciously excluding unacceptable thoughts, feelings, or desires from our minds so as not to act upon them and thereby invite an attack. Children learn what provokes their parents and can carefully avoid those behaviors as a way to avoid punishment.

- *Anticipation.* This involves expecting a positive and mutually satisfying resolution to the problem. Children who can anticipate a change of heart in their parents have hope that things will get better soon. That makes the moment more bearable for many children.

Mature defensive strategies are characterized by rationality, self-control, stress reduction, problem solving, compromise, and mutual respect. Most problems arising out of everyday living can be resolved successfully using mature defense techniques.

But if the attacker is unresponsive to these mature defensive efforts to resolve the issue of conflict and intensifies the attack, a more intense defensive effort may be necessary to protect the victim.

2. Crisis Defensive Behaviors. When confronted by a situation of more serious threat to our well-being and which does not respond to reason and appeal, our response is likely to be one of escape, avoidance, or counterattack. These crisis defensive behaviors include:

- *Displacement.* This involves an unconscious shift of emotion, affection, or desire from the original object to a more acceptable or immediate substitute. Children can try to escape the displeasure of their parents, for example, by projecting the anger they feel toward their parents upon a teacher at school or a friend down the street. This lets the child express the emotion while avoiding a retaliatory or punishing response from the parent.

- *Avoidance.* This involves avoiding further contact with the attacker through physical evasion and hiding or mental retreat into fantasy. Disengaging physically or mentally helps insulate and protect the child from harmful actions or hurtful words from an angry parent.

- *Regression.* This involves trying to appease the attacker through reversion to an earlier or less mature, but more acceptable, pattern of feeling or behavior. Children can sometimes defuse the anger of a parent by crying or other infantile behavior that provokes a protective, nurturing response from the parent.

- *Acting Out.* This involves confronting the attacker or physically or verbally expressing the fear, anxiety, stress, anger, and pain of the distressful situation in ways that may be uncomfortable or painful for other people. Acting out can help children manage and relieve their own levels of stress and pain.

In mild to moderate situations of personal threat and crisis, these crisis defense strategies are usually successful in relieving the stress, avoiding the pain, and escaping or surviving the assault.

But if these crisis defensive techniques are ineffective at protecting us from the attacker and the attack intensifies and becomes even more persistent, then an even more dramatic and intense response from us may be required.

3. Neurotic Defensive Behaviors. Neurosis is any of various mental or emotional disorders arising from no apparent wound or sore or life change and involving symptoms such as insecurity, anxiety, depression, and irrational fears. When confronted by extreme situations of assault or deprivation causing more acute pain and discomfort, and mature and crisis defensive strategies are ineffective in bringing relief, then we are likely to turn to more desperate methods to help us cope and survive these more severe threats to our health and well-being. Neurotic defensive behaviors include:

- *Intellectualization.* This involves an unconscious effort to protect ourselves from the emotional stress and anxiety associated with

47

confronting painful personal fears or problems through the process of excessive reasoning. We can depersonalize an experience by abstracting it, thereby taking away its emotional content and effect. To avoid hurt, we avoid feeling. Intellectualization involves focusing solely upon the cognitive content of an experience without consideration of its emotive or affective content.

- *Rationalization.* This involves a conscious effort to devise a self-satisfying, but incorrect, reason for our behavior. We can avoid feelings of guilt and shame for our acts of omission or commission through rationalization, finding an acceptable explanation that will justify these acts to ourselves and others.

- *Repression.* This involves the unconscious exclusion of painful impulses, desires, or fears from the conscious mind. In an effort to avoid guilt, shame, pain, and punishment, children can block any memory or awareness of what distresses them.

- *Reaction Formation.* This involves a defensive mechanism by which an objectionable impulse is expressed in an opposite or contrasting manner. Children can sometimes avoid the wrath, rejection, and punishment of their parents by being physically affectionate when their impulse is to strike out violently against the parent.

- *Hypochondria.* This involves the persistent conviction that one is or is likely to become ill, often involving experiences of real pain when illness is neither present nor likely. We can avoid guilt and accountability through sickness. Sickness is an acceptable excuse for nonperformance of responsibilities or for not performing up to usual standards. Sick children are less likely to be punished by parents.

- *Neurasthenia.* This involves the experience of chronic fatigue and weakness, accompanied by a loss of memory and generalized aches and pains. Not feeling good, feeling sick, and forgetting are often acceptable excuses for not meeting behavioral expectations. Children who find it impossible to please their parents may find it safer to disappoint them rather than displease them. Avoiding responsibility and accountability might help protect the child from an assault.

- *Psychosomatic Illness.* This involves developing a real physical illness in response to emotional stress. Intense feelings that are unsafe being expressed outwardly often find expression through physical symptoms. Verbally assaulted children might develop stomachaches, for example, as if they are being "kicked in the gut!"

- *Conversion Reaction.* This involves impaired sensory or motor functioning without apparent physical cause. Children can develop an impairment in order to protect themselves from being punished because of an unacceptable sensory or motor activity.

- *Dissociative Reactions.* This involves the separation of a group of related psychological activities into autonomously functioning units, and include multiple personality, a condition in which one person exhibits two or more distinctly different personalities, and amnesia, the total or partial blocking of memories concerning certain past events or periods of time.

- *Phobic Reactions.* This involves a dread or morbid fear of some object, person, or situation that serves as a symbolic substitute for the real cause of fear and anxiety.

- *Obsessive-compulsive Behavior.* This involves thinking that is dominated by a feeling, image, or idea, resulting in a behavior that is an attempt to cope with the obsession through some ritualistic act.

In most situations of acute personal threat, these neurotic defensive strategies will effectively bring relief from stress and help us survive the overwhelming situation.

But in some cases of extreme threat, neurotic defensive techniques of survival are not effective in protecting us from being overwhelmed physically and mentally. Situations that threaten our mental and physical survival with extinction, chaos, madness, and death require even more desperate efforts to survive.

4. Psychotic Defensive Behaviors. In situations of extreme abuse or deprivation where our mental and physical health is being seriously threatened, we may have to survive by employing the most desperate of all methods of survival. These psychotic defensive behaviors include:

- *Delusions.* This involves avoiding the stress, fear, and pain of a threatening situation through a false belief held strongly in spite of invalidating evidence. A somatic delusion, for example, is a persistent belief that you have some physical defect, disorder, or disease; that contrary to all evidence, some part of the body is misshapen, unpleasant, revolting, or ugly. A persecutory delusion is a persistent belief that you are being conspired against, cheated, spied upon, followed, poisoned or drugged, maliciously maligned, harassed, or obstructed in the pursuit of life goals. Similarly, grandiose delusions are a persistent belief that you possess some great, but unrecognized talent or insight, or have made some important discovery, or have a special relationship with a prominent person—sometimes having religious content that can lead to a messiah complex.

- *Perceptual Distortions.* This involves avoiding the stress, fear, and pain of a threatening situation by altering one's perceptions of reality to make them less frightening and overwhelming.

- *Denial of Reality.* This involves avoiding the pain, fear, and stress of a threatening situation through the denial of reality by means of mental illness, such as schizophrenia, any of a group of psychotic disorders usually characterized by withdrawal from reality, illogical patterns of thinking, delusions (false beliefs) and hallucinations (false perceptions), and accompanied in varying degrees by other emotional, behavioral, and intellectual disturbances. Another example is dementia, the impairment of long- and short-term memory associated with impairment in abstract thinking, impaired judgment, personality change, or impairment of other critical higher functions. Delirium describes the reduced ability to maintain attention to external stimuli and to appropriately shift attention to new stimuli, and disorganized thinking as manifested by rambling, irrelevant, or incoherent speech.

In order to maintain a mental health balance, we must believe that we have some power and control over our lives and destiny— that we have the ability to take care of our survival needs, if necessary, and to manipulate our environment in such a way as to get our needs met. *We must have congenital hope!*

When congenital hope is overwhelmed and depleted and our congenital despair becomes acute so that we feel totally helpless, powerless, and out of control, we may turn to the most desperate, and fatal, effort of all to survive.

Let me describe the process using a stress model. Imagine being placed alone in a small closet with no exit but the door you entered. Imagine that there is a guard at the door who will not let you leave, regardless of what you say or do. You are trapped and imprisoned against your will. Another person has taken total control of your life. How will you cope and handle the situation?

Most likely you will go through a process called "psychological regression," which is nothing more or less than an increasingly more primitive (desperate) effort to restore physical and mental control and balance in your life. Everything you do will be an effort to be free of your confinement in the closet and to regain control of your life. You might first try, for example, to reason your way past the guard and out of the closet, perhaps using your negotiation and problem-solving skills while trying to make light of the situation using humor (mature defensive behaviors). But what if these efforts fail to gain your release? Your next level of regression—more serious behaviors designed to regain your freedom and control of your life—might be to challenge the right and authority of the guard to detain you, rant and rave, and threaten the guard with reprisals if he does not release you (crisis defensive behaviors).

But again, what if these efforts fail to convince the guard to let you go? Then your next level of regression might be to try to buy or manipulate your way out. You might offer money or a willingness to do whatever is demanded by the guard in exchange for your freedom. You might become sick or disturbed or apathetic (neurotic defensive behaviors). And once more, what if these desperate efforts to please the guard are not sufficient to bring your release? Your next level of regression—still trying to gain control, power, and balance in your life—might be to act out violently against the guard in the delusion that you can force him to let you out (psychotic defensive behavior). Each step in the regressive process is more desperate, irrational, and dramatic as you attempt to restore mental, physical, emotional, and spiritual health by overcoming, placating, appeasing, manipulating, or escaping your captor.

If all else fails in your regressive efforts to restore freedom and control of your life, if you cannot overcome or escape the life-threatening situation, then your last and most desperate resort is to exert final control over your life and destiny: suicide or madness. You see, the ultimate physical regression is death because *it extinguishes reality.* The ultimate regression psychologically is insanity because *it denies reality.* In either case, you protect yourself from being overwhelmed and destroyed by the attacker.

Being immature, uneducated, and less capable of protecting themselves from those who would do them harm, abused children most often learn to survive in three basic ways: by physically or mentally running away from the attacker through retreat or denial, physically or mentally avoiding the attacker through evasive, manipulating strategies, or physically and mentally hiding from the attacker behind defense mechanisms. If mature and crisis defensive measures do not protect them enough from the abuser and abuse, then abused children may have to become neurotic or psychotic in order to survive.

Abused children often are punished when they behave normally, so they must learn to behave abnormally in order to avoid punishment.

It's an ironic twist that abused children must sometimes make themselves mentally sick to stay emotionally well, must act up physically to settle down emotionally, must run away in order to stay where they are, and must make themselves emotionally dead in order to physically survive.

Why We Behave
the Way We Do

People behave the way they do for a reason. Even people who abuse children. Whether right or wrong, appropriate or inappropriate, rational or irrational, all human behavior is motivated toward one of two basic life-enhancing goals: to avoid pain or to experience pleasure. Pain includes any kind of physical, mental, emotional, or spiritual discomfort. This includes feelings such as physical pain, emotional hurt, distress, anger, irritation, depression, anxiety, fear, dread, stress, need, loneliness, helplessness, and frustration. Pleasure includes all forms of physical, mental, emotional, and spiritual stimulation that makes us feel good. This includes feelings such as happiness, fulfillment, achievement, love, respect, physical pleasure, emotional peace, security, hope, relief, comfort, power, and control.

Survival requires that life be attractive and pleasurable—that our reasons for continuing to live exceed our reasons for ending it. It's the pleasure we derive from life that makes it worth living—the pleasure of family, friends, career, children, service to others. Most people are proactive in their search for life pleasure; that is, we initiate activity that we hope will bring about the desired pleasurable results in our lives. We look for fulfillment in our emotional activities, meaning in our cognitive activities, satisfaction in our social lives, and peace in our spiritual lives.

Whereas some discomfort can motivate us to grow and change, survival requires that we avoid excessive pain. Too much pain can overwhelm our desire or ability to continue living. Most people are reactive when it comes to avoiding pain; that is, we react to whatever is causing us pain by trying to escape or avoid it.

To understand human behavior, we must first understand the reason behind our actions and reactions.

Understanding Human Behavior

All human behavior—even the physical, emotional, or sexual abuse of a child—originates in the brain as the result of a conscious or unconscious thought or series of thoughts. Thoughts stimulate feelings, and feelings motivate behavior. When I have not eaten in awhile, for example, thinking about my favorite food makes me feel hungry. The discomfort of feeling hungry motivates me to seek relief by getting up and going to the kitchen to get something to eat. The process looks like this:

$$\text{THINK} \longrightarrow \text{FEEL} \longrightarrow \text{BEHAVE}$$

Have you ever heard someone say, "The more I think about it, the madder I feel, the more I want to tell him off!" or "You need to think about what you're doing!" or "Thinking about it only upsets me!" or "I don't want to ruin my day by thinking about it"? These are statements most of us have made at one time or another. In them, we're acknowledging that we feel and act the way we do (or would like to) because of what we're thinking.

What we think about ourselves is called self-image. This is what we *think* we are as persons, as husbands and wives, sons and daughters, males and females, and so on. A lot of human behavior is rooted in our need to prove to ourselves or to others that we *are* what we believe ourselves to be, or conversely, that we are *not* what we believe ourselves to be. If you think you're physically attractive, for example, then you'll probably spend a great deal of time, energy, and perhaps money, dressing and grooming yourself in a way that will highlight your beauty. On the other hand, if you believe yourself to be unattractive, you will likely spend less time and effort on your grooming.

Children must initially rely on adults to interpret and define reality for them. As a result, parents can create destructive and dangerous self-images for their children. If you tell children they are bad, stupid, ugly, or worthless long enough, eventually they will believe you. Why would a parent, someone who is supposed to love you, lie to you? Especially about something so important? Children trust their parents to tell the truth.

Children grow up mirroring the image they see reflected in the actions and words of others. They have no other way of knowing who and what they are as persons. They look at the faces of their parents and the people around them and, in those faces, see reflections of themselves. When the mirror is clear, loving and accepting, they see themselves realistically: their beauty, strength, and goodness— what's right with them as well as what might be wrong with them. But when the mirror is cracked, soiled, and stained by anger and rejection, the image reflected back to the child is often ugly and distorted. The tragedy for many children is that they don't know that the distorted image is caused by the crack in the mirror, not by something in themselves. All too quickly children come to believe they are the negative image they see in the mirror of other people's faces. Soon enough they will see themselves as others see them.

Young children tend to believe what their parents tell them— both verbally and nonverbally. They accept what is said as absolute truth. Integrated into their data bank, this piece of "knowledge" becomes a fact upon which they build their view of reality as they struggle to understand life, themselves, and others. They have no reason not to believe and trust their parents. As a result, children must be able to rely on adults to be honest, responsible, mature, humane, and knowledgeable in what they say and do. Too often though, parents are negligent or careless about whether or not what they teach is true about life and themselves. Or, having distorted and faulty beliefs themselves, parents may ignorantly pass them on to their children.

How we *feel* about who and what we are as persons: males or females, sons or daughters, husbands or wives, and so on, is called self-esteem. How we feel about ourselves is determined to a large extent by how others treat us and what we think about ourselves. If I think, for example, that everyone is avoiding me because I am ugly, I am probably not going to feel very attractive. People tend to feel the way they think. Thinking positive thoughts usually evokes positive feelings while thinking negative thoughts evokes negative feelings. Most of us have had the experience of thinking ourselves into a bad mood by dwelling on an unpleasant or upsetting thought. The bad news is that unpleasant things happen to good people every day.

FROM VICTIM TO VICTORY

The good news is that unpleasant events can have pleasant outcomes, depending on how they are handled.

Sometimes, especially as children, we can't control what happens to us or even how we feel about it at the time. What we think and feel about what happens to us can be as punishing as the event itself. The good news is that now as recovering adults we no longer must be victimized by our own thoughts and feelings. *We can control how we think and feel about what happens to us!* Even what happened to us as children. We can reexamine a past event, redefine it in light of what we now know to be true and reintegrate it into our history as just another bad experience we have had to overcome in our lives. We can actually become stronger, saner, more determined, and more valuable to ourselves and others—simply because we were able to survive the abuse and overcome its effects in our lives. At the very least, we can take what we have learned from the abusive experience to educate others and maybe prevent the same thing from happening to another child.

How we act out these thoughts and feelings about ourselves through our *behavior* is called *self-expression.* If I feel unattractive because I think that I'm ugly, then I'm likely to express to others this thought and the feelings it evokes by being withdrawn, impersonal, aloof, and by avoiding personal contact. We communicate our feelings about people by the way we behave toward them. How we behave tells people a lot about us, especially about how we feel about ourselves and them. *People tend to behave the way they feel and feel the way they think!*

To understand human behavior, we must first understand human thinking and feeling. Behavior is a symptom (or expression) of the thoughts and feelings behind it. If I think that I'm unprepared to give a talk, for example, then I'll likely feel anxious and insecure, and those feelings will show in the way I stand and move as I deliver the talk. Expanding the model, it looks like this:

$$\text{self-image} \rightarrow \text{self-esteem} \rightarrow \text{self-expression}$$
$$\uparrow \qquad\qquad \uparrow \qquad\qquad \uparrow$$
$$\text{thought} \rightarrow \text{feeling} \rightarrow \text{behavior}$$

Similarly, how we behave toward others: parents, teachers, and the world around us depends on the esteem we have for them, and that is rooted in the image or concept we possess of them. As an example, if I imagine you to be my friend, I will probably feel good about you and our relationship, and so will behave in an open, relaxed, accepting way toward you. The model looks like this:

self-image	self-esteem	self-expression
mother-image	mother-esteem	mother-expression
father-image	father-esteem	father-expression
teacher-image	teacher-esteem	teacher-expression
world-image	world-esteem	world-expression

think → feel → behave

Thoughts are perceptions arriving at conclusions. Feelings are perceptions and conclusions reacting to other perceptions and conclusions. Behavior is the physical expression of conclusions reacting to other conclusions. Faith is a commitment to our conclusions—about life, ourselves, people, the world, and God.

Our Belief System

The final piece of the puzzle for understanding human behavior is the very root of thinking itself: our belief system. As we think about ourselves, other people, and the world around us, we study them, evaluate them, and then draw conclusions about them. These conclusions are called judgments. The judgments we make affect how we feel and behave toward others.

The judgments we make are also based on our perceptions and understanding of truth and reality. What we believe to be true or false, right or wrong, good or bad, real or unreal will determine what we think, feel, and how we behave in every situation. This behavior will either be reinforced or discouraged, which in turn will strengthen or weaken the beliefs from which they sprang. The process looks like this:

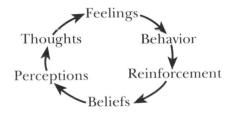

FROM VICTIM TO VICTORY

We build our lives and relationships on reality as we know and understand it. If I believe that you are a good and honest person, then I'll surely think that you are trustworthy, I'll feel good toward you, and I'll likely behave toward you in a friendly, trusting manner. On the other hand, if I believe that you are a thief, then I'll think that you cannot be trusted. I will not feel good about you, and my behavior toward you will probably be to avoid you.

Our belief system is what we believe to be true and real about the world, ourselves, others, and what makes life worthwhile. It comes to us from our parents and other family members, teachers, early life experiences, and television.

Children spontaneously create a theory about themselves and their environment that enables them to fulfill their needs more effectively than if they had, each moment, to rediscover the nature of the world. These theories—beliefs about themselves, others, and the world—include many facts concerning those objects they encounter in their daily lives. People, too, are objects to children at first, and thus they create beliefs about them based upon the facts they learn through encounters with them. But because children's minds are immature and unable to evaluate their beliefs properly until adolescence, they may develop inaccurate beliefs about themselves, their parents, and their environment. Because children's behaviors are based upon their perceptions of the world, which are encapsulated in their beliefs about it, these inaccurate beliefs will gravely hinder their ability to function adequately and will likely cause them to behave in ways that interfere with their growth and development rather than aid their ability to satisfy themselves and others.

These inaccurate beliefs may include such "facts" as that they are unlovable, ugly, stupid, incapable of learning or doing anything right, or that the world is a hostile, dangerous place and people cannot be trusted. Believing any of these "facts" causes great emotional and spiritual discomfort in a child. Believing that they are unlovable, for example, may cause children to avoid people for fear of rejection. The result can be an emotional estrangement from others that leads to painful loneliness and contributes to congenital despair.

Our beliefs about who and what we are and the people and world around us are formed early in life. They become the bedrock of our personality, the firm foundation upon which we build our view of reality and which underlies all our activities. Were we to reject these beliefs, we would have no stable perspective from which to interpret our experiences and to interact with the world. It's the terrifying and pervasive fear that occurs when one has no rational structure within which to understand and order his experiences that is communicated in the word *madness*. Rather than experience emotional chaos, we tend to distort our experiences to fit our existent beliefs rather than reject the belief.

Our beliefs determine the emphasis we place on various aspects of life and different events. Belief does not necessarily refer to religion. Religious faith is but one part of the belief system.

Every action, every choice we make follows from our belief system. Our beliefs are the core of us. They make us unique. No two people have exactly the same belief system. Our belief system is the source of our strength, our commitment, motivation, and inspiration. It is the most precious and private part of us. It can also be the most vulnerable part of us.

Our belief system comprises our changing answers to the ultimate questions of life. Those questions include the following:

1. What is the aim of my life? (my goals) Goals are what we want and hope to achieve. They help us decide how to spend our time and energy. Goals are motivators. They give purpose to life and help us select the actions we are willing to take to fulfill them—and ourselves. Some goals are very concrete and specific. Others are more vague and philosophical. Trouble arises when we do not know what our goals are, when we do not work toward our goals, and when we have too many or conflicting goals. Aimlessness, having no goals, causes us to move from one meaningless event to another. It can also cause us to make bad choices and wrong decisions by default.

2. What is important to me? (my values) Our values define what is important in our lives—our top priorities. Like goals, they can be measured to some extent by the energy we invest in fulfilling them.

Values may be more difficult to identify than goals. They work under the surface, propelling us to act, to make choices, and to move toward our goals. Values and actions are inseparable. By examining our actions, we may discover what we really value. By examining our values, we may better understand why we act the way we do. Generally our actions reflect our values. If you value privacy, you will resent intrusions and disturbances. If you return a wallet you have found, you value honesty. Values are powerful motivators to action. Trouble arises when we ignore our values and do not act on them or when we have conflicting or unclear values.

3. What do I believe? (my faith) Everyone has faith in something. Faith helps us deal with the ambiguities and mysteries of life. It fills the gaps in our information system. We formulate our faith at an early age. Like our bedroom, these beliefs become comfortable and familiar. They help us make sense of the world around us. Our actions are based in part on our faith. If you believe that God has a plan for the world and your life, you may face adversity with confidence and trust, knowing that God is in control. If you believe that you are your brother's keeper, you will look for opportunities to lend a helping hand. If you assume others will be inconsiderate, you will concentrate on protecting yourself. If you believe in forgiveness, you will be more gentle with yourself and others when you or they make mistakes or fail to measure up.

4. Who am I, anyway? (my self-image) Our self-image is a special collection of assumptions and beliefs about ourselves—beliefs about our limitations, our abilities, our appearance, our emotional resources, our place in the world, our potential and worthiness. These self-views, which were learned in childhood and later reinforced through accumulated life experience, give continuity to our lives, providing a framework from which to respond appropriately to the multitude of choices we face daily.

Our self-image tends to be based more on belief than on objective fact! It does not necessarily correspond accurately to external reality. Whatever you believe about yourself is "true" for you and will be a powerful determiner of your actions. If you believe that you are inferior to others, for example, you will probably defeat yourself.

Most people cling tenaciously to their odd collection of beliefs about themselves, even when the facts and feedback from others contradict their self-image. If your self-image is too rigid, it will discount feedback from others. If you cling to the belief that you're stupid, you will reject the gift of respect from others who value your ideas and opinions. Your self-image may also stop you from realizing your full potential. If you believe that you cannot run a mile, you probably will not try. Or if you believe that you cannot get the job, you most likely will not even apply for it!

Our belief system is the blueprint from which we construct our lifestyle. Since our lifestyle choices determine who and what we will encounter in our daily lives, our beliefs are the root of our happiness as well as our problems.

To understand human behavior, we need to examine, evaluate, affirm, discard, and reconcile the beliefs that are of central importance to us. These beliefs are the underlying source of behavior because they have guided us as we carved out our lifestyle from the hundreds of choices available to us every day.

Just as a belief system supports us, it can also tear us down. Serious emotional and spiritual problems occur when our beliefs are irrational, inaccurate, or outdated. If I believe, for example, that mistakes are catastrophic, I may escalate minor troubles into major crises or I may expend too much energy trying to be perfect. I will have problems if I learned as a child not to talk to strangers and carry that belief into adulthood and on to my first job. Outdated childhood beliefs can impair our adjustment and functioning in adult situations.

We build our lives and relationships upon what we believe to be true. But what would happen if we were wrong? If what we thought was true was not true at all! What kind of life could we have if we built it on a faulty belief system? What if you had grown up believing, for example, that stealing was acceptable as long as you did not get caught? Building your life on this faulty belief would likely result in spending part of your life in jail.

Faulty beliefs lead to impaired thinking. When our thinking is impaired, we cannot make sound judgments, which leads to inappropriate feelings and behavior.

Abused children tend to internalize the responsibility for their own victimization, as well as the belief system of their abusers. It is a system of lies, deceit, half-truths, illusions, and delusions. Yet, it is this pool of misinformation and faulty judgments that forms the database for abused children—the knowledge base upon which future decisions will be based.

Faulty Beliefs

Just as it's possible to teach children a positive belief system that will enhance their lives and set them up for success, it's equally possible to teach children a faulty belief system that will diminish their lives and set them up for failure. For example, consider a family where the parents believe education is unimportant. They have no books or magazines in the house and show no interest in the schooling of their children. If this is what the parents believe is true about education, what will their children likely think about education once they become school aged? They most likely will believe, like their parents, that going to school is unimportant. If children believe this, how will they feel when we make them go sit in a classroom against their will? Probably frustrated and angry. How will they behave if they feel frustrated and angry in school? Probably in a way that will prove to both you and themselves that they do not belong in school! People tend to behave in ways consistent with their belief system. We all know that children who do not graduate are at highest risk for unemployment. Because the parents passed their belief that education is unimportant on to their children, those children's future is in jeopardy because of their lack of education. These children have been inadvertently set up to fail!

If children believe that they are unlovable, they will likely think they are undeserving of love or that something is so wrong with them that no one could possibly love them. The core feeling of children like this is usually emptiness and loneliness—a loneliness that aches to the very core of each child. Core feelings of emptiness and loneliness tend to express themselves in self-destructive behaviors—behaviors designed to punish the self for being so bad no one can love them. These can include self-mutilation, promiscuity, anorexia or bulimia, drugs and alcohol ingestion, and other high-risk behaviors.

If children believe that they are inadequate, that no matter how hard they try, it won't be good enough to win approval and acceptance, they will likely think that they are incompetent and undeserving of acceptance. The core feelings of these children are likely to be anger and frustration, expressed in aggressive acting out behavior toward people and things. This behavior can include fighting, vandalism, shoplifting, disobedience, and defiance.

If children believe that they are not as good as other people, that they are somehow flawed and inferior to others, they are likely to think that there is something wrong with them that cannot be corrected, making them unworthy of the same rights and privileges of others. The core feeling of children like this is usually helplessness and despair. Core feelings of helplessness and despair tend to express themselves in apathetic behavior, an "I don't care!" posture toward life and relationships. These behaviors can include a passive response to challenges, an unwillingness to try and compete, a "care less" attitude about their appearance, health, and life in general.

If children believe that they are failures, that they are incapable of doing anything right, they are likely to think that they are worthless to themselves and others and so unworthy of affection and acceptance. The core feeling of these children is shame and guilt: shame for being flawed and guilt for not being able to live up to expectations. Core feelings of shame and guilt tend to be expressed in escape behaviors, behaviors designed to run away and hide from one's own deficiencies. These can include running away, excessive day-dreaming, television, video, reading, and even escape into drugs and alcohol.

Finally, if children believe that they are impotent and powerless to change life or themselves in order to make it more acceptable, they likely will believe that they have no control over their lives and have no real choices. The core feelings of these children will likely be feelings of entrapment and hopelessness. Core feelings of hopelessness and entrapment often express themselves in violent behavior toward others or themselves: in homicide or suicide.

Treating or controlling the behavior will not solve the problem. The behavior is just a symptom of the faulty belief system. There will not be a permanent change in behavior until there is first a permanent change in the belief system. And yet, *the belief system is the hardest thing about any human being to change!* Once we believe that something is true—especially about ourselves—it's incredibly difficult to change our minds. It can take years of therapy and re-education to change just one faulty belief. Or it may never change, depending upon how rigid and protected the belief system, or what role that faulty belief plays in our survival. Belief systems are most amenable to change in people who desire a change in their lives, recognizing that something is not right with them.

Abused children grow up with not just one, but many faulty beliefs about themselves, their parents, other people, and the world around them. Let's identify some of the more common faulty beliefs of abused children:

I AM . . .	PEOPLE ARE . . .	THE WORLD IS . . .
ugly	selfish	scary
not good enough	out to get me	out of control
guilty	out of control	chaotic
unattractive	untrustworthy	undependable
stupid	greedy	unsafe
flawed	superior	overwhelming
helpless	uncaring	toxic
worthless	cruel	alien
dirty	liars	unmanageable
crazy	unpredictable	doomed
unlovable	prejudiced	unforgiving

Let's consider just one simple, faulty belief from this list. Let's take "I am ugly." If people really believe they are ugly, imagine the impact that belief will have on their thinking about themselves, their relationships, life opportunities, their hope for happiness. Then imagine how those negative, pessimistic thoughts will affect their self-esteem, by being a primary force in how they feel about themselves and the world around them. Finally, imagine how those ugly thoughts and feelings about themselves will affect the way they behave toward themselves and others. Many parents don't realize that it is much easier to deflate a child's ego than it is to inflate it. We can bring a child down a notch with just a few words, but to raise a child's self-esteem could take weeks, months, or even years! The impact of just one faulty belief on a child can be profound!

Most human behavior is an expression of personal values and beliefs. For example, for a child to be physically abused, there must be an adult who "believes" that it is OK to hit children—otherwise the adult would not do it. People tend to behave in ways consistent with their belief system. Similarly, for a child to be sexually abused, there must be an adult who "believes" that it is OK to expose children to adult sexuality—otherwise, the adult would not do it! Many children are abused because parents convince themselves that what they are doing is justifiable parental behavior and not harmful to the child.

My Own Faulty Belief System

My belief system was fashioned for me by the people and events I experienced in my world as a child. Though I learned much from what was said to me, I learned even more from the way people behaved. Actions really do speak louder than words! Here are some of the more important faulty beliefs I held as a child growing up:

1. Life is what you do while you're waiting to die. I learned as a child that life is something that happens to people whether they like it or not. It's here for awhile and then it's gone. It's not something over which we have any real control. For some, life is good. For others, it's bad. I believed that the content and quality of one's life is determined not by choice and hard work, but by chance, fate, luck, being in the right place at the right time or being in the wrong place at the wrong time. Some people were just lucky enough to have money, nice homes, clothes, good families, and happiness. I wasn't that lucky. I thought that I had nothing to lose because I could not see what I had. It's easy to take risks when you have nothing to lose. To me, "living" meant to play out the hand life had dealt me. Fate controlled my destiny. My goal was to find what pleasures I could along the way.

2. The goal of life is to feel good. I learned as a child that life is a daily struggle against pain, hurt, and bad feelings. Successful people are those who can make themselves feel good. My primary goal in life was to feel good. I believed that pain and discomfort should be avoided at all costs. Every day and in every way I must do whatever is necessary to make myself feel good, to escape life's stresses and pressures. I came to believe that the normal life cycles of emotional highs and lows can be controlled with drugs and alcohol, or other intense personal experiences, to create the desired mood change. I also learned that I should ignore the pain, guilt, and shame I felt about how I made myself feel better.

3. Do unto others before they do unto you. I grew up to believe that people are basically bad. They are selfish, untrustworthy, and can be very mean when you don't give them what they want. The only way to survive is to be meaner and tougher than other people. I had to be tough, no matter where I was, who I was with, or what I was doing. I had to be able to take it as well as dish it out. I was supposed to always fight back and not let anyone take advantage of me. Retaliation was essential. Taking risks was acceptable. But the best way to survive and get what you want is to act first, to be on the offensive, to do unto others before they can do it to you. Suppression of natural inhibitions and fear was a normal part of everyday life.

4. The ends justify the means. I also learned as a child that life is a constant battle between those who have and those who have not. Those who have not must use any means necessary to get what they want. Lying, stealing, sneaking are all OK if they achieve their goal. They aren't wrong unless you get caught. Taking care of myself meant finding effective ways to get what I wanted and thought I needed.

A fellow survivor, deeply involved in her own recovery, expressed it so well. She said, "What was most important in life was that I get my needs met, not how I do it. If my body is the only thing attractive enough about me to attract and hold the love and attention I craved, then having indiscriminate sex was OK."

5. I have to take care of myself because nobody else will. There were times as a child when I thought that life would overwhelm me and I would go crazy! It seemed that everybody was out to take care of themselves first. I learned that if I was going to get what I wanted, then I would have to take care of myself. I would have to put me first. No one else would help me, so I had to help myself in the most effective, immediate ways possible. Taking care of myself meant avoiding anything painful and uncomfortable. It meant nurturing myself by avoiding reality and responsibility.

Again, this friend said it best when she told me, "When I became an adolescent, I learned that my skill was sex, my talent was conning people to get what I wanted, my special ability was beating the system and not getting caught. My reward was excitement, achievement, and a drug-induced high. I made myself feel good. At least at first. I came to believe that commitment to addiction is commitment to self-fulfillment."

Like her, I believed that everybody has a right to get what they want and need. Therefore, getting what I wanted was the right thing to do, regardless of how I did it!

6. Taking care of myself means making myself feel good and getting what I want when I want it. Taking care of myself came to mean not only feeding and clothing myself, but sedating myself when necessary to ease the pain inside me, rationalizing my behaviors to avoid guilt and shame, blaming others for all my problems and doing whatever was necessary to survive. I learned that objects and events can make me feel good. People usually made me feel bad. They would often judge me, criticize, and punish me. They would use me and take from me what they wanted. And they would use lies and words to manipulate me. At an early age I learned that people can't be trusted to mean what they say, to really care about me, to be concerned about my needs, or to see that my needs are met. Too often as a child, I would turn to an adult for comfort when I was hurting and unhappy and only be rejected. Or ask for something I wanted and be cursed. Or reach out for a hug and be pushed away. Or seek kindness and understanding only to be punished. People were too busy to care very much about me, it seemed. I couldn't count on them to be there for me. Instead, I learned to put my trust in objects and events. Cigarettes became my best friend. Drugs and alcohol became my playmates. I learned to trust and depend on the effects they had on me. They never let me down and were more accessible to me than were my parents.

As I became an adolescent, people and relationships became temporary and disposable. Things were more important than people. I learned to seek intimacy through an object or event. They could make me feel good when I felt bad. I learned to be attracted to objects and events that can bring pleasure. I came to believe that happiness, wholeness, and fulfillment can come through objects and events. Things can make me happy. I also learned that objects and events can bring stability in my life and can help me stay in control of how I feel. People cannot, or will not, give what is needed. People are inconsistent and cannot be trusted.

7. Something is wrong with me and there's nothing I can do about it. School and other constructive activities were for kids who had everything—whose lives were already comfortable and fulfilled. School didn't make me feel good. It only made me feel worse by daily reminding me of my inadequacies: poor performance, dress, social acceptance, friends, and so on. I was incapable of achieving what seemed to come so easily to other children. I had no talents or special abilities. I didn't know anything and I was incapable of learning. I believed that I was inferior to other people. I was "second hand" because the clothes I wore were "second hand." I confused my poverty with me! I learned to measure my worth by what I had—which wasn't much.

8. I'm helpless, but I must control my feelings. I had unrealistic fears and insecurities. I wanted to sleep with someone who would protect me. Normal childhood fears and anxieties were confirmed for me, not relieved. I learned to blame everybody but myself. It was the way I was raised or the way we lived or the way my parents treated me that made me the way I was. I refused to assume responsibility for my actions. I learned that what's most important is being in control of how you feel so that you don't appear vulnerable. You can't be concerned with long-term effects of choices when immediate needs are so neglected and desperate. Drugs and alcohol gave me a way to control my feelings. As did violence. So I would turn to them during crises, high-risk times, times when I felt most out of control.

9. The rules are suspended for me. Once again, my friend said it best. "I was taught as a child that the rules were suspended for me because of my poverty. Poor people cannot buy what they want and need. Stealing was the only way that I could have what others had and I wanted. It was only fair." This is an attitude of entitlement. Because I was deprived as a child, I was entitled to preferential treatment as an adult, I thought. Or at the very least, I should not be held to the same standard of performance and conduct as others.

10. It's OK for bad people to do bad things because that's what bad people do. It's OK to live the lifestyle of an addict, for example, because that's the normal way addicts live! Cursing, fighting, stealing, lying were all status-enhancing behaviors. I wanted to look good so that I could feel good about myself. Besides, only bad people have bad feelings. And I certainly had my share of bad feelings.

11. Bad things happen to bad people. I grew up believing that bad things happen only to bad people. So when something bad happens, it's because you're bad. I internalized responsibility for the bad things which were done to me, believing that I deserved them because I was so bad.

12. I'm a mistake, something that should never have happened. Feeling unloved and unwanted, I grew up believing that I was worthless, a burden to my parents and teachers. I wouldn't ask anything of anyone for fear of burdening them more—even to the point where they would abandon me. I did not belong anywhere. I just didn't seem to fit.

It doesn't take much to see how damaging these faulty beliefs can be, how they can inhibit and impair a child's growth and development. It is the faulty beliefs that are the root of our problems as adult survivors of abuse. Each one is like an abscessed tooth that will not allow us to eat the nutritious food we need to grow and develop normally. And like the abscessed tooth, each one must be located, removed, and replaced. Recovery from child abuse involves seeking, embracing, and accepting the truth, for only in truth is there hope.

The Damaging Effects of Abuse

In addition to physical assault and neglect, there are three very common parenting practices that can seriously impair children mentally, emotionally, and spiritually: double binds, shame, and betrayal. These parental actions, most often done in ignorance, do not just hurt children, but can impede their growth, development, and adjustment.

Double Binds

A *double bind* is a no-win situation that occurs when inescapable, contradictory demands are made on a child. Satisfying one demand ignores the other. This places the child at risk for punishment or rejection. Regardless of which choice is made, it will be wrong or inadequate, and will likely result in suffering for the child. Double binds result in a psychological impasse—creating internal, emotional, mental, and spiritual conflict for which there is no satisfactory solution. A good example of a double bind is what children face when their parents divorce and use the children to control, manipulate, or punish the ex-spouse. Children naturally love and need both parents. To put them in the position of having to choose one parent over another or to protect one parent from the other or to feel that they are somehow betraying one parent if they love the other is cruel and inhumane. Such is the nature of the double bind. Extraordinary coping methods must be developed by the child to deal with the internal conflict and intense emotions that result.

A double bind also occurs for children, for example, when parents threaten children with a spanking if they do not tell the truth and then spank the children for what they have done after they tell the truth. There is no way for the children to avoid or escape the spanking. As parents, we must be careful not be punish our children for being honest in our effort to hold them accountable for their behavior. If we punish children for being normal, we will likely raise abnormal children! Punishing children when they tell the truth often teaches them that being honest is not safe.

My own experience in an abusive family taught me that it was not safe for me to express my true feelings about what was happening to me. Even though I had strong, often overwhelming feelings of fear, anger, and pain, to express them around my parents would only invite more abuse from them. I learned early that my survival depended on keeping still and staying quiet, maintaining an outer complacent composure while inwardly seething with emotions. Such strong emotions don't just go away! If I could not express them around my parents, what was I to do with them? Most often, I had to swallow them, burying them deep inside so that nobody could see them and then punish me for having them. Occasionally I would feel safe enough in a situation outside the family that I could begin expressing some of the repressed rage and pain. But too often, this would get me into trouble at school and with other authority figures.

Those children who were beaten, battered, assaulted, cursed, starved, molested, and raped in homes all over this country last night have some very strong feelings about what happened to them. But most of them have learned that it is not safe being honest about what was done to them last night or how they feel about it.

There is an axiom in auto mechanics which suggests that if you do not pay to have the oil changed in the engine of your car regularly, then you will be paying a mechanic to repair your engine sooner or later. Maintaining an automobile means that you "pay me now or pay me later"! What it costs to change the oil regularly is a great deal less than what it costs to repair an engine.

This same axiom holds true in human psychology: "Tell me now or tell me later!" Those children who were abused last night will either tell us today how they feel about what happened to them last night in ways that are basically harmless—albeit uncomfortable—to us and themselves, or we can deny them that opportunity and force them to repress those powerful emotions. If we ignore their feelings today, they may be able to control them for awhile, maybe even years. But sooner or later, those children are going to tell us how they really feel about what was done to them at home last night. It usually happens when suddenly the children are as big as us, can run, shout, curse, and hit as well as we can, when suddenly they are adolescents and now have the power to do to us what was done to them years before. They will force us to stop whatever we are doing to look at them, to hear what they have to say, and to personally feel their anger, rage, and contempt. It is a scene being acted out in communities all over this country—angry young people forcing innocent society to experience firsthand their pain and anger for having been abused as children.

We will meet those children who were physically, emotionally, and sexually abused in our neighborhoods last night. If we do not meet them in our churches and classrooms, we will meet them on the street when they assault, rob, rape, or kill us. If we do not meet them there, we will likely meet them in our own families some day, when they grow up to marry our sons and daughters and become the mothers and fathers of our grandchildren. But meet them we will!

The mental and emotional harm of the double binds forced upon children by abuse is dramatic. Young children know instinctively, for example, that their survival depends upon the good will of their parents. Most children must please their parents in order to be accepted, cared for, and protected by them. This means that they must remain physically, emotionally, mentally, and spiritually intimate with their parents, totally vulnerable, blindly trusting that the parents will not harm them and will provide them what is needed to survive.

What happens, then, to naive, trusting, and vulnerable young children, driven instinctually to be close to their parents in total trust, when the parent bites them, curses, ridicules, criticizes, slaps, burns, punches, kicks, hits, strangles, and beats them, or fondles, molests, or rapes them, so that now survival demands that the child not be intimate, not trust and be vulnerable to the parent upon whom they must rely for survival? The dilemma for children looks like this:

FROM VICTIM TO VICTORY

1. Survival requires that children:
   - trust the parents with their lives and welfare
   - remain physically intimate with parents
   - stay emotionally and spiritually connected to parents
   - repect the authority of the parents and allow them to be in control
   - submit to the will of the parents
   - be open and honest
   - love the parents

2. But because of the abuse, survival demands that they:
   - not trust the parents with their lives and welfare
   - keep physical distance from parents
   - emotionally and spiritually insulated from parents
   - take control of their lives in order to protect themselves
   - rebel against the will of the abuser
   - hide their true feelings
   - hate the parents for what they are doing

These are just a few of the emotional dilemmas faced by children who are abused. They are all contradictory demands of survival imposed upon the child—double binds. It is impossible to do both at the same time.

Double binds result in irresolvable internal emotional, mental, and spiritual conflict—conflict that cannot be resolved using ordinary coping strategies. Since the conflict and the distress it provokes cannot be resolved, it must be tolerated or escaped. Victims must develop emotional or psychological symptoms to either repress or deny the conflict and express the distress. The only other alternative is to split into two people, so that both demands for survival can be achieved. One self can love and be submissive to the abuser as demanded, for example, while the other self can hate and rebel against the abuser. Whenever reality is repressed, distorted, or denied or we are forced to cope with abnormal demands through extraordinary methods, mental and emotional health is impaired.

Double binds don't just hurt our children; they impair their mental health. Most of the emotional and mental health problems faced by survivors of child abuse are rooted in the double binds forced upon them by the abuse at the hands of the abuser. The moral imperatives we are taught and by which we judge our feelings and actions often aggravate the situation and impede recovery. The victimization of battered women is perpetuated rather than resolved, for example, when they are told by well-meaning counselors to submit to the authority of their abusive husbands and let God take care of the husbands. Or when severely abused children are told that they "should" love and forgive the abuser, or "ought" to talk about what happened and report the abuse, or "must" forget it and get on with their lives. Sometimes how people react to the abuse is as damaging to the child as the abuse itself!

Resolving the conflicting impulses of love/hate, attraction/repulsion, respect/contempt, trust/distrust, buried for years perhaps, and the ethical or moral judgments we make about them, is an important part of the recovery process. Validating the thoughts, feelings, and behavior of abuse victims as being "normal" and "appropriate" for someone who has been abused can be a first step in authenticating both the victim and their experiences.

Shame and Guilt

Have you ever heard a parent say to a child, "You should be ashamed of yourself!"? Most of us have.

We make a serious mistake as parents when we shame our children. Children tend to believe what their parents tell them. If we tell our children that they should be ashamed of themselves enough times, they will likely believe us and become ashamed of themselves.

Once we breed shame into a child's psychology, we run the risk of creating what John Bradshaw calls a "shame-based personality" or an addictive personality or both.[1]

Guilt and shame are emotions often confused in our culture. Guilt is a sense of self-reproach, a remorseful awareness of having done or said something wrong, or for being inadequate. Shame, on the other hand, is a painful feeling of unworthiness and disgrace about who and what we are as persons. We feel guilty about things—things we say and do or don't say and do. We don't feel ashamed of things, but of ourselves—as men and women, husbands and wives, sons and daughters. Children learn early that they can change the things they say and do to relieve their guilt and win the respect, love, and approval of others. But they also learn early that there is little, if anything, they can do to change who they are as persons in order to make themselves more attractive and acceptable to their parents.

They have control over what makes them feel guilty but are powerless to overcome their shame.

Guilt is an appropriate human emotion even for children—when it motivates us to assume responsibility for what we have said and done, or not said and done, apologize and make amends, learn from the mistake, and not repeat the same offense again. Shame is never an appropriate emotion for children. Whereas guilt tells us that there is something wrong with what we have said or done (or not said and done), that we have made a mistake that needs correction, shame tells us that there is something wrong with us that needs punishing, that we are the mistake, and there is nothing we can do to correct it. Children can control and change behavior, but they cannot change themselves. Guilt can empower and motivate persons to assume responsibility for their actions. Shame disables persons, overwhelming them with feelings of incompetence and self-doubt.

Feeling victimized by the actions of others, shame-based persons feel incapable of assuming responsibility for their actions because there is nothing they can do to change themselves.

People who have a shame-based personality will probably spend the better part of the rest of their lives trying to prove to themselves and others either that they *are* the shameful people they believe themselves to be or that they are *not* the shameful people they believe themselves to be. Neither life focus is conducive to happiness and personal fulfillment.

Shaming children not only runs the risk of creating shame-based personalities, it also breeds helplessness into children's psychology—a helplessness that affects their worthiness to be loved, respected, and accepted by others. Once helplessness is introduced into a child's psychology, we have planted the seeds of the addictive personality. One way to understand addiction is as a desperate attempt to make ourselves feel better when we feel bad. Once we discover that we are helpless to help ourselves—to soothe, comfort, and find relief from within ourselves when we feel bad—then we will likely turn out of ourselves for relief. The environment we live in provides many substitute methods for relieving pain and discomfort. Many of those are addictive.

Personally, I have always been haunted by a fear of exposure, that there was something about me that must stay hidden, a badness that would exile me from others if they ever discovered it. My fear has been that if people scrutinized me too closely they would see my badness, imperfections, flaws, scars, and reject me. So I have worked hard over the years trying desperately to not attract attention, of never standing still too long or allowing myself to be studied, analyzed, or examined. I have avoided letting people get too close for fear they would get to know the "real me." I have been afraid of what people might find! Even today I feel safest when I am invisible. Why have I felt this way about myself, you ask? Because of shame. I have been ashamed of myself. Ashamed for being so bad my parents "had" to beat me, for being so flawed that no one could want me, for being so unattractive that no one could love me. Especially for being a disappointment to my parents, for not being what they wanted me to be. The most common mental illness today is depression. The most common cause of nonorganic depression is the helplessness and hopelessness that accompany shame. Shame for what? For not being what somebody thinks we ought to be. In essence, I was ashamed for not being perfect, for being human.

Shame is one of the leading emotional cripplers of children and adolescents. Most often rooted in faulty beliefs about ourselves, it is the breeding ground of low self-esteem, a distorted self-image, feelings of unworthiness, inadequacy, unlovableness, and incompetence. Shame is the reason most of us are not what we could be. A major part of the recovery process is to overcome our shame, to find acceptance and wholeness in the love of God, ourselves, and others.

Betrayal

I have spent the better part of my adult life looking for things like love, justice, beauty, and perfection. I have found beauty and perfection in nature—in rocks, trees, sunrises, sunsets, the wind, and running water. After all, when is a tree perfect? When it's a tree! When it's everything it was created to be. When is a rock perfect? When it is fully itself—a rock! But these standards of perfection do not apply to human beings, do they?

To be perfect as a human being means that we be unblemished, undamaged, unspoiled, spotless, and pure. This is an impossible task because human beings are imperfect by our very nature. Most of us are painfully aware of our impurities, scars, and blemishes. But doesn't that description of *perfect* describe the trust of a newborn infant for his parents? Isn't that a perfect trust? Unblemished?

Undamaged? Unspoiled? Spotless and pure? I don't think human beings can approach perfection in relationships any closer than that which exists between newborn children and their parents or caretakers. It is perfect vulnerability in perfect trust.

Too often, though, new parents do not realize that every relationship the child will ever have—relationships that require trust, intimacy, and commitment—will be affected by how well we protect and nurture that initial trust relationship between parent or caregiver and child. If that relationship is protected, consistent, nurtured, and is safe, the child will probably grow into an adolescent and young adult who can trust, enter into intimate relationships, and make commitments, all of which are keys to successful marriages. But the one thing that will cripple, damage, impair a child's ability to trust quicker than anything else that can be done to them is betrayal! Those of you who have known betrayal in your life know what I'm talking about. It could take years, if ever, to overcome the handicapping effects of betrayal.

It is not uncommon for abused children to develop an attachment disorder—an inability or unwillingness to trust in intimate relationships. Often this results in delay in conscience, social, and cognitive development. It is in early childhood relationships that we acquire an understanding of "cause and effect," the root of rational, logical thought; that we come to know the difference between right and wrong, the root of conscience; and that we experience mutuality and reciprocity, give and take, the root of successful social interaction.

Abused children are betrayed children, betrayed at the most basic level of all human relationships, that relationship upon which they must depend for survival, their parents. To be fulfilled, people must live in relationships within community. They must be able to know and experience the warmth, caring, and acceptance of others and to offer their caring in return. This is especially true for children. Who can they trust to not hurt them, to truly have their best interests in mind, if not their own parents?

As an adult, part of my recovery has been learning not only how to trust once again, but whom to trust and when. Not everyone is trustworthy. I have had to learn to be selective in my relationships, allowing only those persons into my world who will enhance my life by their presence rather than diminish it in their parting. People who have accepted themselves enough that they can accept me. People I can care about and trust to care about me.

Part of my recovery has also been to realize the price of caring. If we are going to extend our hand in love and caring to another, we must expect to have a nail driven through it occasionally. But for every hand not taken, there are many others who take the offered hand and return the kindness. For in touching others, we are touched.

Double binds, shame, and betrayal of trust do not just hurt children; they impair their ability to grow into well-adjusted adults. Double binds impair mental health. Shame impairs self-esteem and emotional health. Betrayal impairs our faith and spiritual health.

Recovery from child abuse is successful, in part, to the extent we are able to resolve the conflicting impulses of love and hate for the abuser, overcome our shame with a restructured self-image and restored self-esteem, and regain the ability to trust—especially ourselves. In recovery we find hope—a hope that comes from a renewed faith in ourselves, others, the world around us, and in the love and benevolence of God.

Self-defeating Roles

Children growing up in abusive families often assume a particular role or function in the family. A "role" is the characteristic and expected social behavior of an individual. Over time, roles can evolve into rigid and controlling behavior patterns. In functional families, members assuming their places in the family and all doing their part helps the family function smoothly and to the benefit of all. But in dysfunctional families, members quietly playing their roles only make the dysfunction worse by continuing to hide the truth. There are certain rules that govern dysfunctional families:[2]

Be Blind: Ignore the bad things happening in the family, deny your own perceptions of reality, overlook parental distortions and denial of truth, fact, and reality, and ignore the role reversal, the mixed messages, and unhappiness.

Be Quiet: Do not confront or speak the truth of what is happening, be loyal to the family and keep its secrets, do not discuss the family's problems, and do not express how you really feel.

Be Numb: Do not feel what you don't see and don't discuss, accept and don't feel the pain when personal boundaries are violated or ignored; the best way to "not hurt" is to "not feel."

Be Careful: You must stay in control so that you do not speak what is not to be spoken or see what is not to be seen or do what is not to be done; you must be alert and vigilant at all times because your environment is hazardous.

Be Good: To be "a good kid" means to be perfect, to never inconvenience, embarrass, or disappoint parents, never have personal needs or express personal thoughts or feelings, be able to mind-read the wishes of parents and do things correctly without instruction, obey the parent in all matters, joyfully, instantly, and perfectly, and don't remember anything but the good times.

When physical and sexual boundaries are ignored and violated in children, for example, it is expected that the children will soften the boundary edges and ignore the pain of violation, numb and deny their feelings about what is being done to them, be blind to their own perceptions and ignore the conclusions they have reached about what is happening, accept the violator's explanation as truth, and be quiet about the entire event.

Roles help us know what to do in threatening situations, protect us from exposure to criticism and punishment for noncompliance, and allow us to hide our real selves, our true thoughts and feelings behind the mask of our role. It's a way to take care of ourselves.

The roles abused children play in their dysfunctional family usually represents the extreme—an exaggeration—of a healthy and normal impulse. As children, these roles are a blessing that help them survive childhood. But as adults, they can be a burden that interferes with success and happiness. Typically, abused children assume one or more of the following self-defeating roles:[3]

1. Caretakers. The caretaker role for children evolves out of role reversal, that is, when parents turn to children to meet adult emotional and physical needs, expecting children to take care of them and to make them feel better.

Children who have assumed the role of caretaker in the family have learned that their job is to take care of the feelings of others, that their value lies in service to the needs of family members. But, too often, they do not learn how to take care of their own needs. They are at least risk for assault, punishment, and rejection when they are making other family members feel better. Caretakers tend to be the most sensitive child in the family, the one whose feelings are easily and often hurt. They are sensitive to any tension in the family and do whatever is necessary to dissipate it.

As adults, caretakers need to surround themselves with needy, dependent people, but tend to keep emotionally distant and aloof from them. They have a need to "fix" and "rescue" other people from their bad feelings. They appear selfless and needless, too busy caring for others to need care themselves. They tend to attract people who will use them. They then feel used and unappreciated because no one is taking care of them as they are taking care of others. They unconsciously discourage in others what they need most from them. They long for real intimacy and closeness, but fear it. They tend to live lonely, estranged lives of silent emptiness, needing so desperately what they fear the most—the love, acceptance, and attention of others.

While it is true that it "is better to give than to receive," it is also true that "God helps those who help themselves." Mental, emotional, and spiritual health requires that a balance be maintained between giving and receiving. It is better to give out of our abundance than out of our emptiness. Imagine a cup filling to the brim until it spills over into the cups around it. Not only does the cup remain full, but it also aids in filling the cups of others. Caregivers must learn to allow their own cups to be filled so that their giving to others will occur in the abundance of their love and caring—out of their overflowing joy and desire—rather than out of their hungry need to be needed.

To see if you have assumed the role of caretaker in your family, ask yourself the following questions:

— Is it my job to keep everybody happy? Do I feel responsible when they are not happy?
— Do I try to "bend the rules" to bail people out of trouble they brought on themselves, to help them avoid the natural consequences of their actions?
— Do I wonder why so many people lean on me and expect me to help them without caring for my own needs once in a while?
— Is it easier to take care of others when they feel bad than it is to take care of myself when I feel bad?
— Does it seem like I never have enough time to accomplish what I want to do because I am busy helping others?
— Am I more interested in talking about other people's problems than my own?
— Do I feel used and unappreciated by other people a lot?

— Do I feel uncomfortable and useless when everybody is happy and no one seems to need me?

2. People Pleasers. The people pleaser role for children evolves in families where there is a strong parent dominance and punitive style of family management. Children learn that they are inherently bad and must please others to overcome their badness. These children have learned that their survival, welfare, and self-esteem is built on never making anyone angry or giving them a reason to punish them. They are obedient, always submitting to the will and fancy of those more powerful than they. They are hiders. They must hide who they are and what they think and feel. Nor can they say no. To do so would be to risk exposure of their badness and the punishment of abandonment they deserve. The only way they can feel safe is to please others. They must be careful not to do or say anything that will offend or make people go away. Then they would be punished or left alone, their badness confirmed.

As adults, people pleasers almost never have satisfying relationships because they tend to be deceitful—directly and indirectly. They are afraid to be honest with what they really think and feel, or what they have done or not done, fearing rejection. They are so desperate for love, acceptance, and affection that they will avoid doing or saying anything that might give someone a reason to reject, punish, or not like them. They appear to have no opinions, preferences, or thoughts of their own.

People pleasers tend to not get what they want and need out of life and relationships, and are afraid to ask for it. Rather than coming straight out and declaring who they are, what they think and feel, and what they want, they hope and pray that somehow others will just "know" and then "care" enough to supply what they want and respect them for who they are. The result is that people pleasers are almost always in a state of emotional starvation. As they starve, they indirectly punish others for not giving them what they will not ask for.

People pleasers also tend to give up their own personal power and cannot claim their basic human rights. They learned as children to stay physically detached and emotionally insulated so that they cannot be hurt by what they cannot control around them. They try to avoid attention and escape scrutiny. Being the center of attention is the same as getting caught and prompts feelings of shame and fear. Because they tend to be uninvolved and passive, others often make decisions for them. To make their own decisions would mean to be visible and risk rejection, punishment, or abandonment. They often end up marrying abusers. People who will not assume control of their lives and assert their rights will certainly find someone willing to take control for them.

People pleasers need to establish boundaries that separate them from others and enforce them, recognizing where others' "rights" end and theirs begin. They need to learn assertiveness, to write and accept a "personal bill of rights" and insist that their rights as human beings be recognized and respected. Most especially, they need to take possession of their own minds, bodies, and spirits—as well as their lives—accepting responsibility for them and claiming as their own the rewards they bring.

Assessment questions:

— Am I afraid that people will not like me or want to be around me if they ever got to know the "real me"?
— Do I have a hard time asking for help from others?
— Do I have trouble saying no even when I know I should and really want to?
— Do I often say "it really doesn't matter" when I am hurt or disappointed—when it really does?
— Do I rarely feel angry but often feel hurt?
— Do I try to avoid talking about problems in order to keep the peace?
— Do I usually feel that the needs and opinions of other people are more important than mine?
— Do I often apologize—even for things I did not do or had no control over?
— Would I rather give in than make someone mad?

3. Martyrs. Children who assume the martyr role in the family have come to believe that they are bad and deserve to be punished. It is a role that evolves out of parents blaming children for all their problems. Martyrs usually become family scapegoats, believing that they are the source of everybody's pain and troubles, that they are bad, unlovable, and just a "bad seed" deserving punishment. Since they are the problem, the solution is to sacrifice their own happiness, comfort, and well-being in order to protect other family members from themselves and one another. It is their job to take on the burden of other family members' problems, to take their punishment, and to protect others by redirecting anger upon themselves.

As adults, their lives may only have meaning and value in suffering. As long as they are suffering, they feel useful and life has meaning. They are fulfilling their destiny. So they may encourage suffering around them and court pain for the sake of feeling normal. Relief from their shame and guilt comes through punishment. They can atone for the disappointment and distress they cause their parents by suffering punishment at their hands. Only after punishment can they be "good" enough to be loved and accepted by the parents. They may even provoke punishment in order to protect others in the family or to "get what they deserve"—punishment—so that they can "get what they want"—love and acceptance.

People tend to accomplish what they truly believe. Since martyrs truly believe that life is supposed to be a struggle, a struggle is what they make of life!

Martyrs need to realize that usually people create their own problems and their own pain. They are not responsible for the feelings of others. Real healing and recovery is only possible when people are allowed to assume responsibility for the consequences of their actions or inactions. It is true that suffering is an intense experience and is an assurance that we are alive, but so is joy, happiness, and peace of mind. Martyrs need to be exposed to other aspects of life which give it meaning and to seek a new, or perhaps just another, purpose for living in them.

Assessment questions:

— Is it my job to protect people from the anger of others?
— Am I usually willing to do without so that others can have what they want?
— Does it feel natural to worry a lot about other people?
— Is my first impulse to say no when an opportunity to have fun comes along?
— Is my second impulse to wonder why I should pass up a good time?
— When things are going well, do I begin to anticipate disaster, waiting for the other shoe to drop?
— Do I believe that life is a struggle and I should accept suffering as my destiny?

— Do I feel guilty or self-conscious when someone praises me or rewards me—as though I don't really deserve it?

4. Rebels. Like martyrs, rebels grow up believing that they are bad and deserve punishment. But unlike the martyr, the rebel tends to fight back. Whereas the other roles try to avoid attracting attention in order to avoid abuse, this role often intentionally draws attention to itself. These children are constantly in trouble, it seems.

The rebel is the child who outwardly expresses the anger, frustration, and helplessness everyone else in the family feels, but dares not discuss. They fight back when they feel wronged and speak up to challenge the denial in the family and often pay the price of becoming the target of the parent's anger as a result. Unlike the other roles that were supposed to lessen the turbulence and stabilize the family, the emotional honesty of the rebels draws attention to themselves and provokes a strong reaction in other family members. The punishing reactions of family members only confirm what the rebels already know—that they are bad and deserve punishment. To further prove this, it is likely that they will act out their pain and anger in school and in relationships. It is also likely that they will have contact with juvenile intervention services and institutions or to try to numb their feelings with drugs and alcohol.

Whereas anger offered protection against hurt as a child, as an adult it only serves as a wall to keep love, affection, and tenderness from getting in or out. Anger masks vulnerability by taking the offensive—the best defense is a good offense. It may be simmering under the surface waiting to be triggered by the slightest aggravation. As a result, rebels may try to provoke conflict as a way to express their repressed rage.

Rebels must learn to channel their anger into constructive avenues—like social causes—rather than striking out randomly, and allow themselves to feel the pain and vulnerability that lurk beneath their tough exteriors. Those who do not learn to channel their anger into socially acceptable causes may continue to act it out in violent or antisocial activities. Unable to feel compassion for those less powerful than themselves, they may continue to punish others the same way they were punished as children. Unconsciously they may have identified more closely with the aggressor than the victim. If they continue to act out as an adult, they invite other authority figures (e.g., police) to control them.

Assessment questions:

— Do I feel that I have terrible luck—that nothing ever goes my way?
— Do I feel that other people are out to use or abuse me, so I have to be tough and do to them before they do to me?
— Do I feel angry and frustrated most of the time?
— Do I sometimes pick fights for no apparent reason?
— Am I suspicious of people, always wondering if they have an ulterior motive?
— Am I afraid that I will lose control of my anger a lot?
— Have I been in trouble with juvenile and law enforcement officials a lot?
— Do I feel like the world is unjust and unfair?

5. Workaholics. Children who assume a workaholic role in the family have been driven to perform by parents. They have learned that their value to the family is in terms of what they can accomplish physically. They have learned to base their self-esteem on activity—not on productivity, just activity. They have to be busy doing something most of the time. It's not who they are or what they think that is important—it's what they are doing at the time. Workaholic children have learned to buy their parents' approval and acceptance, as well as to avoid abuse, by doing things that are pleasing to the parents.

As adults, they may find it difficult to relax and enjoy themselves. They feel uncomfortable when idle and only feel worthwhile when busy, but they can never do enough. They often feel unappreciated when others do not value their activity or accuse them of being too involved in their work. In relationships they tend to communicate that what they are doing is more important than the relationship.

Workaholics need to get their priorities straight, recognizing that people are more important than what they do, lives are more important than achievements, and that quality is the measure of value in most things in life, not quantity. They must learn to relax, to strive for a healthy balance of play and work. Sometimes it is what you do not say or do that is most important to others.

Assessment questions:

— Do I rarely feel that I accomplish enough?
— When I relax or am idle, do I feel more guilt than pleasure?

— Do I move quickly on to another project without celebrating the completion of the first?
— Do people seem to be in my way a lot?
— Do I value work time more than personal free time?
— Do I feel intimidated by unfinished business?
— Do I spend more time, energy, and effort on projects than on relationships?

6. Perfectionists. The perfectionist role for children evolves out of hypercritical parents who continually find fault with their children and demand perfection. Mistakes are the result of a character defect, and are crimes to be punished. Children base their self-esteem not only on how much they can do but how well. Winning and being the best is everything. Mistakes are intolerable and must be avoided. When they do occur, they tend to be taken very seriously. Perfectionists tend to be tense, rigid, serious, and determined. Often, they are overachievers, but find little satisfaction in their successes.

As adults, perfectionists are never really happy because perfection is not possible. They base their self-esteem on the impossible—never being wrong or out of control. They live in a terrible bondage to an impossible standard.

Things as well as people around them must meet the highest standards—always. They are masters at finding fault. Nothing is ever quite good enough. They cannot accept themselves or others as they are, so they must always strive to be "better," always becoming, never just "being."

Perfectionists try to avoid attention while managing the family so as to relieve tension, conflict, and chaos by providing some structure and consistency. They grow up too fast, taking on adult roles, responsibilities, and worries before they are physically or emotionally ready. They are constantly tense and anxious, ever vigilant and alert to trouble that might threaten the family.

Perfectionists may be successful in their professions, but are usually haunted by disturbing feelings of uncertainty and nagging self-doubts. They feel inwardly that no matter what they achieve, it will never be good enough because they believe that they are never good enough. They may look good to others, but don't feel good to themselves. The fear of being discovered makes them constantly tense and anxious. The fear is that someday people will discover that they are not who they appear to be and really are not as competent as they seem. So it's better to keep their distance in relationships, to always stay a bit aloof, than to let someone get too close and discover their fears, uncertainties, and inadequacies.

Whereas the pursuit of excellence is admirable and the dogged determination has a lot to do with their success, there must be a healthy balance of play, rest, and socializing if their lives are to be fulfilled and satisfying. Perfectionists need to learn to accept life—and themselves—as they really are rather than always trying to make them what they should or ought to be. Mental and emotional health can be measured by the extent we embrace reality.

Assessment questions:

— Am I often amazed at the incompetence and inadequacy of others?
— Do I feel out of control when things are out of place?
— Do I find unpredictability unpleasant and intolerable?
— Do I have a burning need to see things put right, said right, done right?
— Do I worry a lot about why I haven't done better?
— Is any kind of personal failure the worst that could happen to me?
— Does it seem to me that standards are slipping everywhere?
— Am I afraid of spontaneity?

7. The Shadowboxers. The shadowboxers are the children who cannot sit still, physically or emotionally. They are here one minute, gone the next. They will not take a stand on anything. They are constantly on the move, darting, dashing, ducking responsibility, attention, conflict—anything that will bring them accountability and cause them pain. It is a role that evolves out of experiencing betrayal by parents and the shame of always being "wrong," "bad," "sick," "inappropriate," or a "problem" for the family. They base their self-esteem on "staying loose." They have learned to never make a full commitment—to flow with the tide, roll with the punches. They cannot give a straight answer—always sidestepping or running through back doors.

As adults, they often have not just one primary relationship but several, so that if one doesn't work out they can fall back on others. They get high living "on the edge" of life, the law, and in relationships. The danger of getting caught thrills them. Life is a game of hide and seek.

They tend to relate best to caretakers who try to "fix it" and people pleasers who blame themselves for what's wrong with them. Guilt and shame have taught them that "if people knew the real me, they would know all the terrible things I have done and what a terrible person I am. I can't let them know the real me."

Shadowboxers are afraid they will show their ignorance by saying the wrong thing, so they don't want to be asked questions. They are afraid of showing their incompetence by doing, so they do not want to be asked to do something. They are afraid to show their inabilities by trying, so they do not want to try. They are afraid of failure. The best way to avoid failure is to avoid taking risks.

Shadowboxers need to realize that there are few all-right or all-wrong answers in this world. Most things are a little of both, a little more of one than the other perhaps. There is little satisfaction in a life that is estranged and unconnected to others.

Assessment questions:

— Do I find it difficult or impossible to tell people the whole truth, especially about me?
— Would I rather end a primary relationship than make a binding commitment?
— Is figuring out "what I can get away with" or "beating the system" exciting to me?
— Is it foolish to take a stand when there will always be someone trying to prove you wrong?
— Am I afraid that I don't have what it takes to be what people want me to be?

Most of us can find a little of ourselves in each of these behavioral roles. A role becomes dysfunctional when it is our only way of relating to ourselves, others, and the world around us. Roles that bind, control, and enslave us interfere with our growth and development. A healthy balance in all aspects of life is important to maintain health and wholeness.

Learned Patterns of Survival Behavior

Because victims of child abuse must find ways to take care of themselves in often dangerous situations, they may develop particular patterns of thought and behavior that make it easier to survive the abuse.[4]

"I've got to stay in control."

Chaos and uncertainty characterize dysfunctional and abusive families. Children learn to stay alert and vigilant for impending danger, constantly attuned to what is going on in the family. They also learn to deny, suppress, and repress their feelings, thoughts, as well as outward behavior. For some, their survival hinges upon staying in control of themselves, on saying and doing (or not saying and doing) the right thing at the right time.

In my own abusive childhood experience, my parents demanded that I maintain an attitude of "happy cooperation" in all situations and even insisted at times that I "show my gratitude for them loving me enough to correct me" even while they were beating me! Have you ever tried to smile and show affection for someone who is beating you? In order to survive and minimize the abuse, I had to control my thoughts, feelings, and behavior with an iron will. I dared not physically or emotionally express anger, contempt, hate, disrespect, or even hurt—all the things I felt most—for fear of provoking a retaliatory or corrective response from my parents. Even today, I stay very cool in the midst of crises.

"I can't let anything bother me!"

Victims of child abuse learn to deny their feelings, to not trust any of their feelings and ignore whatever their senses tell them. They learn that feelings are to be feared. They are dangerous and can get them into trouble. To not hurt, don't feel. To not feel, don't think about what is happening. Don't risk others hurting you because of the way you feel. The intensity of child abuse can result in an emotional overload that can cause emotional "shut down" to avoid disintegration. Many survivors who learned to emotionally shut down as children to avoid feelings find that it is hard for them to feel intense emotions as an adult.

My first book is called *Cry Out!* I named it that because my parents would not let me cry when I was being beaten. Crying only angered them more and often intensified the attack. Have you ever heard a parent say to a child, "You want to cry? Let me give you something to cry about!"? My parents would sometimes beat me until I was crying and then beat me for crying! In order to survive and minimize the abuse, I had to learn how to desensitize myself to what was being done to me and to the pain it caused. I can still anesthetize parts of my body and block the pain.

"It's all my fault."

Victims of child abuse often feel guilty and ashamed, believing that they are responsible for their parents' actions and for the abuse they and their siblings received. Children are typically self-centered and usually think that the events around them are the direct result of their behavior. As adults, they continue to feel responsible for other people's feelings and actions. If someone is upset, they blame themselves, feel guilty and obligated to do something to take away the upset. If someone is angry, they assume it is because of something they said or did.

For years I blamed myself for the abuse, excusing my parents' behavior, rationalizing it as "discipline" and necessary "correction" for my misdeeds and misbehavior. They told me that they "had no choice," that if I wasn't so bad they would not "have to do it," and that they were hurting me "for my own good" and because they "loved me." And I believed it! Today I do not believe that anymore. I know that my parents were responsible for their behavior just as I am responsible for mine. They did not have to abuse me. They chose to abuse me.

"I don't know what to do! How am I supposed to act?"

Lacking a healthy role model, many victims of child abuse have to guess what it means to be normal and what is appropriate behavior in certain situations. They grow up in an environment of extremes that requires survival behavior. Their goal is not to "get along," "be successful," or "be nice," but to survive. Often they have to watch others and model after them, hoping that *they* know the right thing to do or say. Part of the "reparenting" process involved in recovery may be to learn as adults what should have been taught as children. This can include appropriate manners, grooming, sexual expression, communication, problem solving, and basic life-management skills.

FROM VICTIM TO VICTORY

Whatever success I had as a child and teenager in school and elsewhere resulted from my ability to study others and then model my actions after them. I used to pride myself on my ability to survive new and threatening situations by hiding my real, inadequate, and unacceptable self from people by appearing to be like them. Many of the skills I have learned come from emulating others.

"It's got to be all or nothing."

Survivors of child abuse often think in absolute terms—things are either all right or all wrong, all good or all bad. There is not much of a middle ground in abusive families. You either "do it or else!" Pain is pain and fear is fear. Since things are seldom all right in these families, then they are often all wrong. As adults they tend to trust somebody completely or not at all. People are either acceptable or they're not. There is no in between. They don't realize that success comes in small steps toward a desired goal rather than in one giant leap. There is little value in partial success. If they can't have it all, then it's not worth having. This thinking affects their self-esteem as well: they are either all good or all bad.

In my recovery, I had to deal with my own absolute thinking. What helped me the most to overcome my all-or-nothing attitude was learning how to play chess and then watching the Bobby Fischer/Boris Spassky world chess championship. Bobby Fischer won that championship. He was the best chess player in the world. But I couldn't help noticing that in winning the championship, he lost several matches to his opponent! I came to realize that he was the best in the world not because he won them all, but because he won more than he lost! I learned that to lose a match doesn't mean that you are a bad chess player. It just means that you lost that one match. It also taught me that no matter how good you get at something, there will always be those who are better than you and those who are worse than you on any given day. It also taught me that even a champion can make a mistake that costs him a match. What determines the outcome of a tournament, though, is not what you did to lose the last game, but what you do to win the next game. "Good" people sometimes do "bad" things. But that doesn't mean they are bad people. It just means they did something inappropriate. I learned that success is not winning them all, just winning more than I lose.

Addictions

Survivors of child abuse often develop drug and alcohol problems or addictions of another sort. We seem to be at a higher risk of becoming substance abusers and addicts than those people who have not been abused in childhood. Why is this?

Becoming an Addicted Person

No one is born a drug addict. Most children are afraid of needles and have a hard time taking pills. And few enjoy the taste of alcohol! Yet, the seeds of the addictive personality are often planted early in life—in childhood—at the very time when we are most repulsed by the addictive substances.

It's true that some babies are born addicted to the same drug their mothers used during pregnancy, but these babies are not addicts. They are merely victims of others' addiction. Addicts practice their addiction. Food addicts binge. Gambling addicts bet. Alcoholics drink, and drug addicts take drugs. Babies are incapable of feeding an addiction inherited from their mothers. If left alone, they will either evolve naturally out of their mothers' addiction or die.

This is not to say that addicts are not responsible for the behaviors that lead to their addiction. They are! They choose, for example, to seek out the substances or events that enhance their addiction, to pursue a lifestyle that condones and even encourages the use of drugs and alcohol.

FROM VICTIM TO VICTORY

Why people become alcoholics and drug addicts is no mystery. Alcohol and many drugs are addictive substances. To use them recreationally and frequently is to run the risk of becoming addicted to them. It's that simple!

This doesn't mean that everyone who drinks alcohol or takes prescribed medication will develop an addiction. Most do not. What it does mean is that becoming an addict is not really a matter of personal choice. We choose whether or not to drink alcohol and take drugs, but the natural consequences of those activities are not always a matter of choice. I can choose, for example, to jump off a building, but I can't choose whether or not I fall to the ground. A natural law of physics called "gravity" controls the outcome of that activity!

Anyone who drinks alcohol or takes drugs is at risk of becoming dependent upon them—unable to feel good without them—and developing an addiction to them. The risk for some people is higher than for others, especially if there is a history of addiction in the family. Though I've met many people who choose to drink alcohol and take drugs, I've never met a person who chose to become an alcoholic or drug addict.

The truth is that it's impossible for someone—anyone—to become an alcoholic or drug addict if he or she doesn't drink alcohol or take drugs!

The real mystery is not how we become addicts, but why we choose to practice in excess those behaviors that are at highest risk for developing an unhealthy addiction. We can become addicted to food, sex, exercise, television—almost anything—especially if it is used as a substitute for a basic life need, such as intimacy. It has been said that we can even become addicted to our own adrenaline!

Answering this life-saving question should be a major concern of every parent. The key word is *choose.* Teaching and enabling our children to make wise, healthy choices is one key to protecting them from addictions. We must teach them moderation in all things, to maintain that vital balance of health. But we can't wait until they are adolescents. That may be too late!

Parents are like farmers: the seeds we plant in the spring will be the crop we reap in the fall. To protect children from addictions in adolescence, parents must purposively and systematically plant and nurture the seeds of a nonaddictive personality in early childhood. Although there are no guarantees, there are things we can do and say around our children in their early childhood that will maximize or minimize the probability that our children will develop addictive personalities. Physical, emotional, and sexual assault and neglect in childhood maximize the probability of children growing into addicted adults.

The Addictive Personality

Within all persons at all times are the seeds of health and sickness, strength and weakness, love and hate, right and wrong, faith and doubt. Which of these will become primary personality traits depends to some extent on genetics, and to a large extent upon what is nurtured and rewarded within ourselves, our family, and the environment around us. Medical science has shown, for example, that all of us carry cancer cells within our bodies. As a result, all of us are potential cancer victims. Yet, only some of us actually develop cancer. There appears to be a lifestyle involving how we deal with stress, diet, exercise, and other life maintenance factors that increases the chance of developing cancer.

Similarly, within all persons, at all times, are the seeds of an addictive personality. They are planted through experiences of abuse, hurt, rejection, punishment, betrayal, estrangement, alienation, and feelings of abandonment in important early life relationships. As with cancer, there is a lifestyle that enhances the probability that a child will grow into an addictive personality.

An addictive personality is a person who is at highest risk of developing a physical or psychological dependence upon nicotine, alcohol, drugs, sex, food, gambling, pornography, work, or some other substance or event. Persons with an addictive personality tend to turn to mood-changing substances or activities to make themselves feel better when they feel bad rather than to another person. For the addict, cigarettes, liquor, drugs, food, and sex may be substitutes for the love, acceptance, and intimacy they so desperately want and need but cannot seem to get through meaningful human relationships.

Addiction is a form of nurturing through self-medication and avoidance.

What Is Addiction?

In his book, *The Addictive Personality,* Craig Nakken defines addiction as "a pathological love and trust relationship with an object or event." An addiction is a compulsive physiological or psychological need for a substance (e.g., drugs, food, alcohol) or activity (e.g., gambling, sex, work). The substance or activity is needed to alter the mood of the persons as a way to control their feelings and make themselves feel better. One way to understand addiction is as a desperate attempt to make ourselves feel better when we feel bad.

Addictions don't just happen. They are born out of a desperate need to feel good (safe, clean, secure, loved, wanted, fed, intimate) and to have control over those feelings. Emotional and physical needs often feel urgent and compulsive. The lure of drugs and alcohol and other addictive substances is their promise of relief from discomfort and the power one has to control them.

The Development of an Addiction

Once introduced to drugs and alcohol, for example, some hurting people continue to use them, usually because they make them feel good. Or at least different. At first they seem to work. Unwanted feelings are replaced by others more pleasant. They make us feel euphoric, confident, excited, successful—all the things we don't feel without them. But most important, they give us a way to control our feelings. Always before, everything and everybody—parents, family, friends, teachers—had the power to make us feel bad. And we feel bad about everything most of the time! But with drugs and alcohol, we don't have to feel bad anymore unless we choose to. With them we have the power to alter our mood, to take care of ourselves, to make ourselves feel better when we feel bad, quickly, simply, completely. No one else can control our feelings anymore. We are in control. And that feels good!

When we first use drugs and alcohol, we want to get something out of them: a sense of relief from scary or painful feelings, a sense of euphoria and well-being. We use them only occasionally and in small amounts. At this point we are just a drug and alcohol "user."

As time goes on, though, and our uncomfortable feelings of inadequacy, rejection, powerlessness, and helplessness grow, we turn more and more away from school, activities, and relationships to make us feel good and rely more and more upon drugs and alcohol. They are quicker, more dependable, more accessible, and we know what to expect from them. As our dependence grows and they become our primary source of comfort, intimacy, and excitement, we become a drug and alcohol "abuser." Now our concern is not so much to "get" something from the drugs as it is to "keep" what we have already found.

But then, after a while of steady use, our reason for doing drugs and alcohol changes again. Instead of wanting them to make us feel good, we find ourselves suddenly needing alcohol and drugs to keep from feeling bad! It's like we become allergic to ourselves and need an antiallergen to relieve the allergic symptoms so that we can be comfortable with ourselves. We feel terrible—abnormal—as if something is wrong with us without them. Our body gets sick and hurts. Our heart can't bear the awful feelings of loneliness, shame, and emptiness we feel without them. And our mind can think of little else as it seeks relief. We can't live with or in ourselves without them. Now, suddenly, we need to have drugs and alcohol regularly just to feel normal. We are no longer drug and alcohol "users" or "abusers." Now we are "addicts."

At first we just wanted to change the feelings stirred in us by other people and hurtful events—feelings like fear, rejection, guilt, shame for not pleasing someone or being what they want us to be or doing what they want us to do. But as we become addicted to the "medicine that makes us feel better," our focus changes to needing to stop the feelings that arise from within ourselves—the sickness, the pain and loneliness, the shame and awful emptiness. Instead of wanting to feel good, now all we want is to not feel at all. Drugs and alcohol can help us become numb to those feelings we cannot control without them.

Making Choices

One of the primary reasons young people begin drinking and taking drugs is because of their inability to make wise, healthy choices. Although a journey into addiction involves thousands of choices along the way, the single most important choice involves how we are going to deal with our feelings.

Too often adults forget that children occasionally have intense, powerful, frightening, and sometimes overwhelming feelings that they do not know how to handle—feelings that make them feel sick, bad, weak, or vulnerable; feelings that often bring criticism and punishment if the child tries to express them.

This is especially true for abused children, who often react with powerful, overwhelming and frightening feelings toward the abuser and the abuse, but find it unsafe to express these feelings honestly and naturally. Instead, they are forced by life circumstances to repress these feelings, to turn them inward upon themselves in order to avoid being punished for them. For every act of abuse, there is an intense emotional reaction within the victim.

Whether a child or adult, we have three basic choices when it comes to dealing with our feelings:

1. We can be honest with ourselves and others about how we really feel and why, and then seek healthy ways to express and deal with them.

2. We can ignore and deny our feelings, pretending to the world and ourselves that they do not exist and that everything is fine.

3. We can try to escape our feelings by running away from them through escape behaviors like excessive reading, television, fantasy, eating, or drugs and alcohol.

Who I was as a child and where and how I lived stirred intense emotions in me as did what was being done to me—feelings so strong that I could not ignore them. I had to make choices at a young age about how to deal with those awful feelings brought on by the severe abuse. It's a choice our children will have to make as well. It's a choice we all have to make every day of our lives. But, as a child, I had no idea how to make the right choice! I didn't even know that I had a choice. I basically learned to deal with my strong feelings by watching my family deal with theirs.

Which of the three options above for dealing with feelings would you choose if you believed that:

1. you would be judged, condemned, rejected, and punished for expressing how you really feel?

2. it's a sin to have the feelings you do?

3. it would hurt others you care deeply about if they knew how you really felt?

4. you would be overwhelmed and smothered by your feelings if you expressed, even acknowledged, them?

5. expressing your feelings would only make you want more of what you cannot have?

6. expressing how you really feel would only make things worse?

7. expressing how you really feel would only prove what a bad person you really are?

These are common fears for most abused children. They are also barriers to open, honest communication between parent and child. Children are not free, in many families, to express how they really feel without fear of punishment and rejection or being made to feel guilty for feeling the way they do.

Inexperienced at expressing intense emotion, children are often punished when they express true feelings because parents misinterpret what is happening as disrespect or back talk. Or they feel compelled to punish children when they express bad feelings because "good boys and girls" are not supposed to feel that way.

Because my parents were abusive and I could not trust them to not hurt me when expressing how I really felt, I learned early that I could not express my feelings openly and honestly. At first I attempted not to deal with my feelings at all, to ignore them and hope they would go away. Bad choice! Option #1 was out.

But as time went on, I found that I could not ignore and deny my feelings because they were too strong and intense. I felt so deeply and so constantly that I was in an emotional whirlwind most of the time. Ignoring my feelings was impossible. I chose not to completely ignore my feelings, to at least acknowledge them. Good choice. Option #2 was out.

The only other alternative was for me to find ways to escape my bad feelings, to lessen their effect upon me. This is what I chose to do. Again, bad choice.

I chose to escape my bad feelings by replacing them with other feelings that felt better. Alcohol and drugs, along with other acting-out behaviors such as running away, violence, and sex promised to do that and more. I was seduced by the false sense of control and well-being they offered. I grew to trust them as a friend, to believe in their magic to make me feel good when I felt bad. The good feelings they produced made me feel normal and somehow safe.

I did not know that my bad feelings are normal. I thought that something was wrong with me, that only bad people have bad feelings. Nor did I know that there are healthy, good ways of dealing with bad feelings. I sought relief in the only way I knew—drugs and alcohol, and acting out. They made the pain and hurt go away for a while. I liked that. A lot. Too much.

Decision making is an important skill practiced many times every day. Some choices we make help us; others hurt us. Some make us feel good, and some make us feel bad; some strengthen us or weaken us; some protect or endanger us. Some choices enhance our lives while others diminish them. But with every choice there are gains and losses.

Healthy decision making involves making choices that maximize our gains and minimize our losses—both long- and short-term. Unhealthy choices involve choosing immediate gain while ignoring the cost of future potential losses. How to make appropriate and healthy choices is a skill best taught in childhood.

Drugs and alcohol gave me immediate, short-term relief. But in the long run, they betrayed my trust and robbed me of everything I valued most: my home, family, friends, dignity, self-respect, and almost my life.

Some choices we make today will determine the quality and content of our lives tomorrow! Everything about my life today is the result of choices I made in the past. I would never have suffered from drugs and alcohol, and the consequences of other acting-out behaviors, if I had chosen to say no to them. That was a choice I could have made. But I didn't because my experience with them was not hurtful but instead helpful, it seemed at the time. They made me feel numb when I didn't want to feel anymore. They made me feel safe, confident, important, and most especially, in control of my feelings when I felt most threatened by what I was feeling. I thought that using drugs and alcohol or sex or violence to alter my mood when I felt bad was taking care of myself when no one else would!

Medical science has found cures to many diseases and ways to relieve the debilitating symptoms of many others. It is important that we recognize and accept the healing and relief that prescribed medication can offer, while at the same time remembering that its excesses can be lethal. Seeking medical treatment for medical problems and psychiatric treatment for mental problems is a wise and sound choice. It is an act of maturity and personal responsibility. Maintaining that vital chemical balance within our bodies that is so necessary for health may occasionally require prescribed medication. This should not be confused with drug abuse!

Communicating Feelings

We are not helpless in the face of drug and alcohol problems, violence, gangs, child abuse, crime, and unwanted adolescent pregnancy. Parents have available to them the single most effective tool for protecting themselves and their children from these unnecessary social disasters—if they would just recognize it, accept it, and learn how to use it effectively.

How many of us as teenagers felt something, did something, or wanted to do something we were afraid to talk over with our parents for fear that they would not understand or fear of their rejection, punishment, or of hurting them? If the truth be known, probably most of us! There came a time when we believed that we had to protect ourselves from our parents and our parents from us!

When our children get to the point where they believe that they have to protect us—parents—from adolescent peer pressure, from adolescent temptations and sexuality, from adolescent life and reality—from them—then we have lost our kids. They are now set adrift in a world where they must make critical life decisions—intimate and personal decisions that will affect the rest of their lives—alone. Because they must protect us from what they are thinking, feeling, wanting, and facing because they don't feel comfortable discussing with us the real life issues confronting them, then they must make those decisions alone without the wisdom and guidance of parents who have already lived that part of their own lives and survived it. Their primary source of information, guidance, and support has been cut off because they do not feel comfortable talking to their parents about the most real, sensitive, and critical choices facing them.

When my son was younger, he came in from a date one night and said, "Papa, can I talk to you?"

"Sure, son. What's up?"

His eyes searched my face for a minute as if trying to make up his mind about something. Then he spoke.

"Papa," he said, "Susan and I want to have sex."

Though surprised that he was being so honest and straightforward, I wasn't shocked. Of course they wanted to have sex! They're normal human beings. For parents to think that their adolescent child does not want to have sex would be foolish and irresponsible.

"So . . ." I urged him to continue.

"Well, I know all the reasons why we should go ahead and do it," he explained. "Now will you please tell me why we shouldn't do it?"

I'm serious; he really did ask me this question! Can you imagine an adolescent male feeling so comfortable with his father that he could openly discuss this very important decision in his life? If my son had not been able to talk openly with me, where would he have gone to get his question answered? Who would have given him the information he requested so that he could make an informed, intelligent decision about this most intimate and private part of his life? Probably no one. He would have made his final decision based on what he knew—which were all the reasons why they should go ahead. But because he could openly and honestly talk to me, I was able to give him all the reasons why it was unwise and unsafe for them to have sex at this point in their lives.

The most effective tool we have as parents, to protect our children from incest, abuse, gangs, drugs and alcohol, adolescent pregnancy, and most of the other tragedies that can befall them as young adults, *is an open, honest line of communication where children feel safe and comfortable talking to parents about anything*—anything affecting their lives, without fear of punishment, rejection, preaching, judgment, or criticism.

Parents are their children's primary source of information, guidance, and support as they face the challenges of growing up in a world full of temptations, distractions, and misinformation. Let's not sever that line of communication! Let's not force them to make critical life decisions out of ignorance and lack of information. Let's make sure that line of honest communication remains open and clear. But this can only happen if children feel safe with their parents, that they can be truly honest with what they are really thinking and feeling, to make themselves totally vulnerable to us in absolute trust that we will not hurt, reject, punish, or humiliate them for being honest. It's important that we deal with real life issues using straight talk, imparting important information needed to make wise choices. Good preparation will allow them to make their decisions out of enlightenment rather than ignorance.

Meeting Intimacy Needs

People have needs. Important needs. Sometimes desperate needs. A large part of our daily activity is designed to fulfill our special needs. One way or another, in appropriate or inappropriate, healthy or unhealthy ways, people will find opportunities to get their needs met. Our mental, emotional, and physical health demands that we do! Life depends upon it.

People normally get their emotional and intimacy needs met by reaching out to others—through intimate connection with family members, friends, their community and God. But addicted persons have learned to turn inward, away from people, away from the world and God, to the addiction in order to feel better when they feel bad.

Many survivors of child abuse learn that relationships with others are often too painful to pursue—that instead of bringing relief, they often bring more pain in the form of betrayal, mistrust, conflict, violence, and fear. So they must find another way to meet their emotional and intimacy needs, a way they can control that is accessible and dependable and brings them relief rather than additional torment.

Children have to rely heavily upon their parents to meet their needs, to feed them when they are hungry, for example, and to help them feel better when they are not feeling very good. But if parents cannot or will not help their children feel better, the children must either suffer alone, often in silence, or find a way to make themselves feel better without the help or guidance of the parent. But children have fewer options for providing themselves relief from discomfort than do adults. Turning to events or substances is an easy, accessible, dependable—though often unhealthy—way to do it. A seed of the addictive personality is planted, for example, when children must continually turn to a blanket or stuffed animal (or a bottle) for comfort at night when they are feeling bad (wet, hungry, chapped, frightened, insecure, abandoned) because their parents refuse to pick them up and hold and rock them to sleep for fear of spoiling them.

Too often for victims of abuse, who have learned that primary relationships are hurtful and dangerous and must be avoided, emotional and intimacy needs can only be met by turning to what is available. Tragically, what is most available and least threatening are addictive substances or activities.

Learning to make wise, healthy choices about how to make ourselves feel better when we feel bad is an ability first developed in childhood. How to make unwise, unhealthy choices is an emotional disability also learned in childhood.

FROM VICTIM TO VICTORY

The two most important keys to protecting our children from addictions are:

1. To teach them how to make appropriate, safe, and healthy choices.

2. To identify, evaluate, and select appropriate, safe, and healthy ways to meet their emotional and intimacy needs.

Most people make important life choices based on what they believe to be true about themselves, others, and the world around them. However, these judgments may be inaccurate.

My judgment was impaired in early childhood by an emotional disability called a faulty belief system, which grew out of my early life experiences with my family and the world we lived in. It was an emotional disability that rendered me incapable of making wise, appropriate, and healthy choices.

My recovery has been successful only insofar as I have been able to recognize and overcome my faulty belief system.

Posttraumatic
Stress Disorder
in Victims of Child Abuse

Life is most often remembered as an event—one memorable event after another interwoven into a tapestry of human experiences that we call "our life." Recalling our lives means to remember specific events and their impact upon us. It's the thoughts and feelings they inspire in us that give meaning to the events in our lives and make them worth remembering.

Not all life experiences are remembered years, even days, later. We tend to mentally filter out of our memory the extreme experiences in our lives, particularly those that threaten to bore us to madness or frighten us to death. Ordinary, routine experiences of living are rarely remembered in detail later, unless they're especially pleasant. This time next year, for example, I doubt that I'll remember what brand of cereal I ate for breakfast this morning, or which cologne I chose to wear today, or the color of my socks. These are mundane daily events that have no special meaning to me. They're too boring to remember.

Similarly, extremely frightening events can be so threatening that the only way to survive them is to repress their memory. Even while writing *Cry Out! Inside the Terrifying World of an Abused Child*, which details my own abuse as a child, some of the more bizarre and severe abusive events remained buried in my subconscious and unavailable to my conscious mind. I didn't become conscious of them until years later, when I was more mature, stronger, and better able to deal with them in ways not harmful to myself and others. The brain has the incredible ability to shield us from harm by denying us access to threatening reality until we are mature enough to understand and cope with it. Much mental illness is the result of this natural defense being breached, as when children are taught to swim by throwing them into the water, or when parents force children prematurely to confront their fear of darkness by locking them alone in a dark room.

The only events of my life today that I'll likely remember tomorrow are the ones that stand out from the rest, those events which attract and hold my attention because they're important to me.

Experiences with special meaning are the ones most easily remembered. These are events that fall out of the range of ordinary, daily life routine. They tend to be dramatic, intensely pleasant (or unpleasant), stress-provoking, or events that challenge our understanding of life and threaten our ability to cope. They leave an impression upon us. A year from now, for example, I would certainly remember a phone call telling me that one of my books had been nominated for a Pulitzer Prize, or that I had won the Publisher's Clearinghouse Sweepstakes, or that my son had quarterbacked Tulane University's football team to a national championship! These are all events that would have special meaning for me because they affect important parts of my life. Should they occur, I would surely remember them for the rest of my life!

The more intense the experience, the greater its impact upon us. The deeper the impression, the more likely it is to hurt. Impressions that hurt often leave scars, both physical and emotional. There's a law of physics that tells us every action will have an equal and opposite reaction. There's a similar principle that applies to human psychology: *for every physical action to us there will be an equal emotional reaction within us.* The stronger the action, the stronger our reaction to it. The deeper the impression left upon us by an event, the more likely that it will be indelible, effecting permanent change in us, our thinking, and behavior in the years ahead. There are things that can happen to us that will alter our lives forever. Severe child abuse is an example.

Too often we think of child abuse as those things we say and do to children that "hurt" them. Well, child abuse certainly hurts. Hurts are an inevitable part of every intimate relationship. It's not possible to live in intimacy for very long without there being occasional hurts. But, there's a difference between hurts and severe abuse. The primary difference is that hurts can heal. There's never total recovery from severe child abuse! This is not to say that there can't be total healing. The body can heal given proper medical attention; the mind can heal given proper psychotherapy; and the emotions and spirit can heal given proper counseling, prayer, and support. But the truth of what happened will never change. It will remain a fact in our personal history that will have some effect upon us for the rest of our lives.

Severe child abuse is like taking a precious vase and dropping it on the floor so that it shatters into a hundred pieces. Then we, as clinicians, come along with our clinical glue and begin trying to put the pieces back together again. If we are knowledgeable and skilled enough, when we complete the reconstruction process, we'll have a vase, won't we? But is it the same vase it was before it was broken? No, it is not. And it will never again be that same vase. This doesn't mean that it will be better or worse because of the abusive experience. That will be determined by many other factors. It just means that it will be "different" in the sense that the person has been altered by the experience.

If we are to effectively stop and prevent child abuse, we must acknowledge that child abuse can do more than just hurt children. It can impair them! Impair their ability to think, to feel, to learn, and to socialize. It can impair their physical, mental, and emotional health. It can impair their ability to grow into well-adjusted, successful adults. It can even be lethal. Child abuse doesn't just hurt children; it can impair, cripple, maim, scar, and destroy them.

Stress, Distress, and Trauma

According to Dr. Hans Selye (*Stress Without Distress* [New York: Lippincott, 1974], p. 27), "Stress is the nonspecific response of the mind or body to any demand made upon it." It doesn't matter whether the cause of the stress is pleasant or unpleasant, welcome or unwelcome; both will provoke an adaptive response within us, a response that is out of the ordinary. Winning a million-dollar lottery can be just as stressful as losing your job!

Damaging, unpleasant, or painful stress is called distress. Distress becomes trauma when it's so intense that it threatens to overwhelm our coping capacities. Trauma is an imbalance between the environment and our ability to adapt to its demands. When something in the environment, for example, puts more pressure on your leg than it can bear, the likely result is a broken leg. This is the dynamic at work when we speak of a "broken heart," a "broken will," a "shattered faith," a "splintered mind," or a "fractured ego." Each of these phrases refers to an aspect of the human personality being overwhelmed by life demands. This is trauma.

Traumatic experiences, like child abuse, assault our basic assumptions about life and reality while eroding our trust in ourselves and others. It threatens our ability to cope with the feelings those frightening experiences evoke in us. Abused children tend to lose basic trust in several ways: first, that we are in control of our lives and can take care of ourselves; second, that the world is a rational, safe, and predictable place; third, that people are benevolent and trustworthy; and finally, that we have the ability to bring comfort and relief to ourselves when we feel bad.

The abusive event stands alone in our memories as an unintelligible aberration, a monster, something sinister and foreboding, unintegrated into current or previous life experience. It can't be processed as just another dynamic experience in the flow of human life. It doesn't fit in anywhere. It's so far out of the ordinary realm of human experience that it must be dealt with separately. Ordinary methods of understanding and coping with it are generally inadequate and ineffective. So extraordinary methods must be devised that will reinterpret the event as safe and manageable, or allow us to escape or deny it entirely so that it doesn't totally overwhelm us.

There's nothing sane, safe, ordinary, or rational about child abuse. It traumatizes the victim, challenging the victim's understanding of all things at all levels. Its method is violent, its purpose is disintegration, its effects are disorder and madness. Victims must develop extraordinary coping methods in order to survive not only the abusive event but also life in its aftermath.

People who experience severe trauma are substantially affected by it in some way. The effects can be short- or long-term or permanent. The effects of trauma are generally recognized as symptoms. Usually, the more intense the experience, the more dramatic are the symptoms that result. These symptoms represent the failure of particular psychological functions to deal with the overwhelming experience. They demonstrate the victims' often desperate attempt to cope with what has happened to them and to continue with their lives in spite of it. These symptoms usually begin immediately or soon after the traumatic event. However, it's not uncommon for victims of severe trauma—like child abuse—to begin experiencing symptoms after a latency period of months or years following the experience, though avoidance symptoms are usually present during this period. Posttrauma symptoms can be physical (e.g., nausea), mental (e.g., psychogenic amnesia), emotional (e.g., anxiety), and spiritual (e.g., doubting God's love).

The pain of being abused does not end with the final blow or the last caress. Victims of child abuse typically develop symptoms in response to their life- and health-threatening experiences. Often these symptoms interfere with ordinary life functioning, personal growth, and general well-being. An important part of recovery for victims is to recognize, identify, and find relief from their symptoms.

Posttraumatic Stress Disorder

It is now commonly accepted that following an accident of intense, traumatic experience, a person may develop symptoms of stress or panic disorder. The concept has been labeled "posttraumatic stress disorder" in the psychiatric community. There are numerous examples of posttraumatic stress disorder described in popular and classical literature. The development of workers' compensation benefits during the late nineteenth century is in response to this very concept.

Posttraumatic stress disorder is now recognized by the American Psychiatric Association as a neurotic disorder. As described in the APA's DSM-III-R manual, its essential feature is the development of characteristic symptoms following a psychologically distressing event that is outside the range of usual human experience. The event causing the trauma would be markedly distressing to almost anyone under similar circumstances and is usually experienced with intense fear, terror, and helplessness. A few of the many characteristic symptoms include the following:

1. Reexperiencing the traumatic event through flashbacks, nightmares, and intrusive imagery.

2. Avoidance of people, places, things, or events associated with the trauma.

3. Psychic numbing of emotional responsiveness.

4. Increased physical, emotional, and mental arousal.

Clinically, posttraumatic stress disorder is not diagnosed if the disturbance lasts less than a month.

Sometimes there is a physical component of the trauma, which may involve direct damage to the central nervous system as the result of, for example, malnutrition or head injury. It's common for victims of child abuse to experience more than one type of abuse at the same time. Child abuse affects every aspect of the child.

Though posttraumatic stress disorder can be caused by many kinds of disasters, it appears to be more severe and longer lasting when the trauma is caused by human action or inaction, particularly by family members. Abuse betrays the child's trust in the most basic of all human relationships: the relationship with parents.

Classic symptoms of posttraumatic stress disorder in abuse victims include:

Reexperiencing the Traumatic Event. This can occur in a variety of ways. Commonly the person has recurrent and intrusive recollections of the abusive event or recurrent distressing dreams during which the event is reexperienced. In some instances there are dissociative states, like flashbacks, lasting from a few seconds to days, during which components of the abusive event are relived and the person behaves as though reexperiencing the event at that moment. There is often intense psychological distress when the person is exposed to events that resemble an aspect of the traumatic event or that symbolize it, such as anniversaries.

Persistent Avoidance of Associated Stimuli. The person commonly makes conscious, deliberate efforts to avoid thoughts or feelings about the abusive event and about activities or situations that arouse recollection of it. The avoidance of reminders of the trauma may include psychogenic amnesia, selective forgetting, mental filtering of memories, psychological denial and repression of important aspects of the traumatic event, running away, and self-medication. It's not uncommon for victims to underestimate the severity of their own stress reactions to abuse by assuming that what happened to them isn't as severe or as bad as what may have happened to someone else. Much of the emotional harm caused by abuse stems not so much from the abusive act, but from the moral and ethical judgments that are made about it by the victim, the family, and important others in the child's life.

Too much focus on the survival aspects of the event and not enough on the personal choices made by the victim can interfere with recovery. Victims make choices—out of necessity, to be sure, but choices nonetheless. These choices carry moral judgments and result in consequences. Many victims of abuse have a distorted sense of personal responsibility for their own victimization. The extent of personal blame victims heap upon themselves is determined by the moral judgments they make about their actions and choices in the midst of the abuse. Choices made and actions taken to protect oneself from abuse that results in the abuse of a sibling, for example, will carry more self-blame, guilt, and shame than actions taken to appease the abuser in order to avoid an assault.

Psychic Numbing. Diminished responsiveness to the external world, referred to as "emotional anesthesia," usually begins soon after the traumatic event. It often involves feeling detached or estranged from other people, a loss of interest in activities that previously brought satisfaction and enjoyment, and a decrease in the ability to feel emotions, especially those associated with intimacy, love, tenderness, and sexuality. Victims of child abuse may also experience a sense of a diminished future. They may believe that they will never get well, or be happy, or be married and have children, or have a career, or live a normal life span. They may feel doomed, hopeless, and trapped.

Increased Arousal. Persistent symptoms of increased arousal that were not present before the traumatic event often include: difficulty in falling and staying asleep, hypervigilance, hypersensitivity, hyperactivity, difficulty concentrating and completing tasks, general nervousness, and exaggerated startle response. There may even be changes in levels of aggression. In mild cases this may take the form of irritability accompanied by fears of losing control. In more severe forms, particularly in cases in which the survivor has actually committed acts of violence, the fear of losing control is conscious and pervasive, and the reduced capacity for self-control may express itself in unpredictable explosions of aggressive behavior or an inability to express angry feelings.

Symptoms of posttraumatic stress disorder are often intensified or precipitated when the victim is exposed to situations or activities that resemble or symbolize the original trauma. A female abused by a male, for example, may be bothered by intrusive imagery (memories, flashbacks, nightmares) of the assault. In an effort to protect herself from the bad feelings the intrusive imagery provokes, she may avoid close contact with people and things that may remind her

111

of the assault, in this case, men. The avoidance behavior may reduce the frequency of the intrusive imagery. But she is likely to experience heightened anxiety and even more intrusive imagery, should she find herself inadvertently in close physical contact with a male. In addition, self-imposed estrangement from males can diminish opposite sex intimacy and interaction, and can result in emotional deprivation. The more vivid the intrusive imagery, the more determined the avoidance behavior. This is understandable when we consider that what the victim is trying to avoid is more pain. Avoiding pain is necessary for survival. The dilemma, however, is that to avoid the pain of remembering the abuse through avoidance behaviors, the victim must suffer the pain of estrangement and often the loneliness that comes from disrupted interpersonal relationships. This often leads to feelings of impaired self-esteem, repressed rage, a desire for revenge, impulsive outbursts, difficulty feeling close to family members, and a sense of danger in reinvesting in others.

Depression and Anxiety. Symptoms of depression and anxiety are common in victims of child abuse. The anxiety stems from living in an unpredictable, hostile, and threatening world where the victim must be constantly alert for danger. The depression is often associated with the intense, unexpressed feelings provoked by the abuse, but which the victim believes are not safe to express.

Impulsive Behavior. Impulsive behavior can occur, such as suddenly changing place of residence, unexplained absences, running away, or other sudden and dramatic changes in lifestyle. Personal traumatic episodes, repressed and unexamined for perhaps years, yet still powerfully charged affectively, may result later in sudden, unexplainable, impulsive acts to reenact the abusive event or to avoid any memory of it at all. Often, when there is not an initial working through and resolution of the traumatic experience, the return to normal functioning forces the working through of the traumatic action to take place at the subconscious level. Thus, in many survivors, the playing out of the traumatic action often takes the form of flashbacks, nightmares, impulsive behavior, and unconsciously, but specifically, "undoing" the past and correcting past faults by acting out its opposite in survivors' present lives. Subconscious undoing of the past frequently takes the form of victims' becoming intensely involved in helping other victims.

Organic Mental Disorder. Some victims of child abuse may show symptoms of an organic mental disorder, such as a failing memory, difficulty in concentrating, emotional lability (instability), headaches, and vertigo (dizziness).

"Victims of a devastating trauma may never be the same biologically," said Dr. Dennis Charney, a psychiatrist at Yale University and director of Clinical Neuroscience at the National Center for Post-Traumatic Stress Disorder ("Key to Post-Traumatic Stress Lies in Brain Chemistry," *Voices* [January-February, 1994] p. 9). Scientists are finding that a single instance of overwhelming terror can alter the chemistry of the brain, making people more sensitive to adrenaline surges, even decades later. For brain changes to occur, the stress must be experienced as catastrophic, an overwhelming threat to life or safety, and one over which they have no control. Severe child abuse can be just such an experience!

Guilt and Shame. It is common for survivors of child abuse shared with siblings to experience painful feelings of guilt and shame. They often feel guilty and ashamed for:

- Surviving when a sibling did not.

- Suffering less than one's brothers and sisters.

- The things they had to do and say in order to appease the abuser and survive.

- Not doing enough to protect themselves and their siblings.

- Surrounding disclosure of the abuse and the subsequent trauma of intervention and treatment for the family.

The role of personal action and responsibility in abusive situations is important to consider because most victims of child abuse internalize responsibility for their own victimization. This self-blaming may take the form of perceived personal responsibility for individual actions or for failures to act in the midst of the abuse. The victims are more likely to remember choices that result in hurtful consequences for siblings than heroic actions which may have spared them all more suffering.

Suicide among victims of abuse is often associated with survivor guilt, the sense of having been transformed into a bad person by the abuse, feelings of hopelessness and entrapment, and the fear of repeating the cycle with one's own children. The issues of punishment, reparations, forgiveness, and atonement are central issues in recovery.

FROM VICTIM TO VICTORY

Impairments and Complications. Child abuse forces children to behave abnormally in order to appease the abuser and to develop abnormal strategies for coping with the distress it creates within them. The results can be mental, emotional, and social impairment. The impairment may be either mild or severe and affect nearly every aspect of life. Phobic avoidance of situations or activities resembling the original trauma, for example, may interfere with interpersonal relationships such as marriage or family life. Emotional lability, depression, and guilt may result in self-defeating behaviors or suicidal actions. Victims may learn to survive through passivity—a learned emotional disability.

A potent kind of learning called conditioning takes place in the midst of child abuse. Children learn to respond defensively to a certain stimuli regardless of its level of threat at the moment. This learning takes place in an environment of danger and the need for life-preserving behaviors. It is survival-dependent learning and may be extremely difficult to unlearn.

Flashbacks and Nightmares. Flashbacks are characterized by a sudden reexperiencing of a stressful, traumatic, or frightening situation. They may be precipitated by a sensory experience resembling the original event or by heightened arousal, such as anger, which makes the repressed memories more accessible to the conscious mind. Flashbacks are characterized by a disruption of appropriate sensory processing. Typical anxiety symptoms during flashbacks include:

- Dyspnea (difficulty breathing, shortness of breath)

- Palpitations (irregular, rapid heartbeat)

- Dizziness

- Paresthesia (a skin sensation like itching, burning, prickling, with no apparent cause)

- Chest pains

- Diaphoresis (perspiration)

- Trembling or shaking

- Hot or cold flashes

- Fear of losing control

114

Typical precipitants of flashbacks include environmental reminders, dysphoric mood (an emotional state characterized by anxiety, depression, and restlessness), personal life stress, fatigue, and activities associated with sleep.

Typical perceptual experiences of victims during flashbacks include: seeing faces associated with the traumatic event, perceptual distortions or illusions (e.g., a parental hug perceived as an attempt to sexually seduce), and abnormal perceptions that seemed real at the time but later are doubted or disproved by reality testing.

Like nightmares, flashbacks represent the failure of the mind to interpret, process, and integrate the traumatic event into the flow of one's past and present psychological history. They are a dramatic attempt by the victim to resolve the conflict existing between "normal," satisfying life experiences that the person seeks out and "abnormal," painful life experiences that are forced upon them. Repetitive flashbacks and nightmares may be an attempt at mastering under one's own control events that could not be dealt with originally.

Nightmares are a prominent symptom of the trauma of child abuse. In general, the term *nightmare* refers to the bad dream the sleeper awakens from feeling apprehensive, frightened, and anxious due to painful mental imagery.

Persons suffering from traumatic nightmares usually have experienced disruptions of the self, experiencing a temporary loss of self-cohesion, difficulty in maintaining their self-esteem, and the loss of a sense of well-being in the face of threatened interruptions in their relationships to important people in their lives. They have failed to develop or have traumatically lost their ability to provide a consistent sense of self, maintain their self-esteem, and enable them to soothe, comfort, and bring relief to themselves when they feel bad.

Recent research on sleep and dreaming suggests that dreams may have an adaptive function: dreaming is how the mind processes and integrates life experience and modifies defensive and coping mechanisms in response to current life demands. Dreams portray the struggle between past hopes and present realities. The nightmare is a failed dream, a dream that does not complete the process of integration of present and past experience.

Traumatic nightmares may result from a breakdown of the psychological functions that allow dreams to function as a means of making sense of the day's emotional experiences in light of one's life situation and previous experience.

Survival Belief System. In order to integrate abusive life experiences into their understanding of life in general, victims of child abuse must make judgments about people, themselves, and the world around them. These decisions most often are made in the midst of crisis, when it will directly affect their ability to survive. Some examples of survival judgments might be:

- "I'd better not tell her what I'm really thinking because it might only make her madder!"

- "I'd better do what he tells me to, or he might really hurt me!"

- "If I weren't so stupid, this wouldn't be happening to me!"

Survival judgments are made in the service of survival. But survival judgments, when reinforced, often condense into conclusions and then into beliefs. Notice how the previous observations could develop into the following:

- "It's not safe to be honest about the way I really feel."

- "I'm safe only as long as I please others."

- "People will hurt me if I don't do what they want me to do."

- "I can't trust people not to hurt me."

- "Bad things happen to me because I'm bad."

Survival beliefs may be very appropriate for abusive life situations but totally inappropriate for any others. Because survival is at stake, survival beliefs may be generalized to include all people, all places, and all things. These faulty beliefs are likely to interfere with an accurate perception of life, people, and reality; with our ability to establish and maintain intimate relationships; with our ability to adjust to changing life demands; and with our ability to accept and live with ourselves.

Congenital Hope and Despair. Hope flourishes where peace abides. Peace is a spiritual contentment derived from harmonious relationships free of hostility and conflict, and sustained by mutual good will. Human beings were created not to perpetuate war and conflict but to be at peace. Much of life is spent seeking peace among ourselves and with others. Congenital hope is inspired to the extent peace is achieved. That which sanctifies life gives hope. Love, compassion, mercy, and forgiveness give us hope for humanity—hope for our own redemption, for our deliverance, for a better tomorrow.

Child abuse overwhelms our congenital hope and aggravates our congenital despair. It threatens doom and annihilation, a life of suffering. When congenital hope is overwhelmed by congenital despair, we are doomed, for there is no hope.

Whether the posttraumatic stress disorder is maintained or mastered in the victim of child abuse will be determined largely by the following key factors:

- The strength and appropriateness of their coping responses, that is, whether their responses are adaptive and lead them to deal with the trauma or are maladaptive and lead them to avoid or anesthetize the pain with substances such as drugs and alcohol.

- The extent to which the victim identifies, challenges, tests, corrects, and replaces life protection beliefs with life-enhancing beliefs.

- The victims' ability to make the transition from the reflex of conditioned abuse survival to adaptive, nondestructive expressions of intense feelings in their current lives.

- The extent to which the victims' congenital hope can be refueled so that they can once again dream, plan, and act with purpose and with some confidence that what they are doing is a right and good thing.

- The extent to which they are willing and able to be honest with themselves and others and embrace truth and reality.

- Their willingness to experience the pain of recovery in order to achieve its joy and peace.

- Their willingness to address the spiritual issues of shame, sacrifice, and salvation while pursuing forgiveness for themselves and others.

- And finally, the extent to which they are able to find relief from their symptoms.

The ultimate goal of recovery is not to alter our history by rewriting it, to deny it by wishing it away, to escape it by erasing it from our memory, but to claim it! It is part of who and what we are today.

Recovery means to reclaim what has been lost. What was lost in the abuse was an integrated self; a whole person with a life of possibilities; a life with a past, present, and future. It means to become fully ourselves once again, to find a new reason to trust in a renewed faith in ourselves, others, and the world around us; to once again take pride in our gender and feel its possibilities; and to seize the power that is within us to take charge of the rest of our lives. Ultimately recovery means to interweave our minds, bodies, hearts, and spirits into a complete person, grounded in reality, but inspired by hope of a better tomorrow.

Finding Relief for Symptoms

Most survivors of dysfunctional families experience enough stress and trauma in childhood to develop symptoms in adulthood. The function of symptoms is to help the individuals cope with what they have experienced by finding physical, mental, and emotional outlets for the intense feelings provoked by the trauma. Relieving the symptoms of stress will not solve the problem, but will make them more comfortable while we seek healthy solutions. It is difficult, for example, to teach a person how to grow crops in order to feed his family when he has not eaten for three days. Relieving the immediate stress of hunger first will free his mind to consider long-term goals.

The first step in recovery is to relieve the immediate stress of deprivation that may threaten survival. This includes food, shelter, clothing, transportation, employment, and medical treatment, if needed. There are agencies available to assist in meeting these needs.

The next step is to assess the level of commitment to recovery. There are some people who, frankly, do not want to get well. Some people feel comfortable enough in their lives as they are right now that they do not want to change. They have become so accustomed to living the way they do that change may be frightening. For them, recovery means giving up what they know and are most comfortable with—victimization. It means assuming responsibility for and being held accountable for their lives and behavior. It's easier and less threatening for some to remain victims. Only when the pain of not

119

changing becomes greater than the pain of change will these people take recovery seriously.

Recovery can be a painful experience—at least at first. But there is even greater pain in continued victimization and in living in bondage to an abusive past. Just as there is some discomfort in cleansing and dressing a physical wound, so too, is there some discomfort in treating emotional wounds. Just as a little pain is inflicted with the needle when we receive a shot to prevent the greater pain of sickness and disease, so too, the process of recovery can be uncomfortable as we strive to relieve our suffering.

If you are seriously committed to recovery and can accept the pain of change and the discomfort of embracing reality in anticipation of the joy and peace of mind it can bring, then the next—and perhaps most critical step—is to get control of those behaviors that are out of control and threatening to your life, health, and welfare. This means that you must stop doing what you know is wrong and unhealthy. It also means getting help to control those behaviors that seem beyond your control right now—like drug and alcohol abuse. If you really want to get well, then you will seriously go about the business of recovery. There is only one way to make it happen and that is to just do it! Get up. Get ready. Get help. Get out. And get on with it! You have everything to gain and nothing to lose but your painful memories, the frightening nightmares, that horrible emptiness inside that seems to ache to your very core, and that awful loneliness, not to mention the shame that paralyzes you and leaves you feeling numb.

The rest of your life is worth whatever it takes today and tomorrow to reclaim it! But nothing will be different tomorrow if you don't act today! The rest of your life depends to a large extent upon what you do today, right now, to make it better. And, yes, you do have the power right now within you to begin reshaping your life, to make it into the kind of life that you want it to be. You must be willing to move slowly and patiently, though. Change sometimes takes time. But my recovery, and the recovered lives of thousands of other adult survivors of child abuse, is living testimony to the power of recovery. You have the opportunity to begin the recovery process—right now! You have the power to change within you, it's the same power you used to survive! The only question left is: Do you have the will to recover?[1]

You can begin by working through the following assessment in the privacy of your own heart and mind. Answer these questions as honestly and completely as you can. Be specific. Write down your answers, so that you can refer to them later or record them on audiotape.

Memories

- Are there periods in your life that you cannot remember?
- What is your earliest memory?
- What is your most vivid childhood memory?
- Can you remember "happy" times as a child?
- Do others have memories of your childhood that you do not have?

Motivation

- Are you experiencing any particular problems—physical, mental, emotional, spiritual—that you think are directly related to your abuse as a child? If so, what are they?
- Do you have recurring memories that interfere with your participation in and enjoyment of life? If so, what are the most common ones?
- Do you think that you need help dealing with the abuse and resolving the problems that have resulted?
- Do you feel you have been pushed by others to seek counseling help?
- How do you feel about being offered counseling help?
- Do you have any previous counseling experience or any strong feelings about it?
- How much time each week are you willing to invest in changing your life?

The Trauma Event

- What happened exactly? Take your time and identify as many instances of abuse as you can recall. Describe them in detail.
- Who did it?
- When and where did it happen?
- Who else was involved?
- What (if any) particular memories now interfere with your enjoyment and participation in life and relationships?

- Did you think at the time that you were going to die, get sick, get a disease, or get pregnant?
- Was anyone close to you hurt?
- Were you injured? How? Did you seek medical help?
- How do you think you coped at the time with what happened?
- Sometimes people feel that they have let themselves or someone else down by the way they reacted in a crisis; do you feel that way?
- What is most disturbing about it all for you?

Coping Since the Abuse

- How do you think that you have coped since the abuse?
- How do you feel that you have coped with the unpleasant memories?
- Are some situations now difficult to handle in a way they were not before the abuse?
- Have you ever felt so distressed by what happened that you feel like you can't carry on with the usual activities in your life?
- Do you ever cry or get angry when thinking about it?
- What do you do when you feel overwhelmed by it all?
- What do you do when you feel really angry?
- What do you do when you feel depressed?

Avoidance

- Are there any situations you now avoid because they remind you of the abuse?
- Do you try to avoid certain thoughts or mental pictures related to the abuse? If yes, how?
- Do you try to avoid certain memories?
- Do you ever discuss what happened with anyone?
- Do you try to avoid thinking about it too much?
- Do you sleep a lot?

Intrusion

- Do you have nightmares about certain incidents in your life?
- Do you have nightmares about the abuse? How often in the past week?
- What happens in the nightmare?

- Do you wake up at a certain point?
- How do you feel when you wake up?
- Are your thoughts and mental pictures of the abuse so bad when you are awake during the day that you can think of nothing else? Or are they usually in the back of your mind and you can get on with other things? Or are they there occasionally but don't really bother you?
- Do you experience flashbacks?

Reactivation of Earlier Trauma

- Has what happened to you reminded you of another bad experience in your life?
- Has it awakened earlier, painful memories?
- Have those memories triggered other memories?
- Does it remind you of something that has happened to someone you care about?

Irritability

- Do you find that you are more irritable than before you started dealing with your abuse?
- Do you fly off the handle more?
- Do you get more irritated when others make mistakes?
- Are you more impatient with yourself, spouse, or children?
- To what do you attribute your irritability?
- Do you feel nervous and anxious a lot for no apparent reason?
- Do you feel tense and frustrated more than you used to?
- Do you have a tendency to overreact when you get stressed out?

Neurotic Symptoms

- Do you often have headaches?
- Is your appetite poor?
- Do you sleep badly?
- Are you easily frightened?
- Do your hands shake?
- Do you feel nervous, tense, worried for no real reason?
- Is your digestion poor?
- Do you have trouble thinking clearly?

- Do you feel unhappy?
- Do you cry more than usual?
- Do you find it difficult to enjoy your daily activities?
- Do you find it difficult to make decisions?
- Is your daily work being neglected?
- Have you lost interest in things which before were important to you?
- Do you feel you are a worthless person?
- Have you thought of ending your life?
- Do you feel tired all the time?
- Do you have uncomfortable feelings in your stomach?
- Are you easily tired?
- Do you have a hard time finding humor in life?

Substance Abuse

- Do you smoke? Drink? If so, how much a day?
- Are you on prescribed medication? If so, what?
- Do you use alcohol or drugs to help you cope with your distress?
- Do you feel that alcohol and drug use is a problem for you?
- Do others who are important to you say that your alcohol or drug taking is a problem for them?

Other People's Perceptions

- Looking at the overall circumstances of your life, how stressful do you think most people would regard it as having been:

  not stressful
  mildly stressful
  moderately stressful
  severely stressful
  extremely stressful
  catastrophically stressful

- Why?
- How do you think others—family and friends—perceive you as a person? Your life in general? Your work?

Life Before the Abuse

- How satisfied were you with your life for the year preceding the abuse, if you can remember it?
- Has the abuse made worse any difficulties you were having before the event?
- Did you get into trouble more than most kids your age as a child and teenager?
- Have you had previous trouble with your nerves? If so, how and when?

Suicidal Tendencies

- Have you ever felt that life was not worth living?
- Have you had thoughts of committing suicide?
- Have you ever developed a specific plan for committing suicide?
- Have you ever written a suicide note?
- Have you ever started doing things according to that plan?
- Have you actually made an attempt on your life?

Support

- Do you have anyone that you feel you can talk to about what you have been through?
- How have your friends and family responded to you since the abuse?
- Does your family support your getting help?

After you have answered these questions as thoroughly as you can, or if you have difficulty answering them, and you are ready to *recover*, then it is important that you seek out a licensed couselor or therapist to assist in your recovery efforts. Be careful to find someone you feel confortable with, someone you can trust implicity and who has experience with adult survivors of child abuse. It is important that they supervise your self-help recovery activities.

The three characteristics that most uniquely describe *posttraumatic stress disorder* are: (1) intrusive imagery or thoughts; (2) avoidance reactions; and (3) heightened arousal (restlessness and irritability). The following strategies may help you find some relief from your symptoms.[2]

Intrusive Imagery or Thoughts

These symptoms are a threat to your sense of personal control. The images or thoughts often arise unbidden, unexpectedly, and often at inappropriate times. In extreme cases, they can provoke dissociative episodes (flashbacks) or psychogenic amnesia. There are four basic treatment strategies:

1. Containment. Most people just want to be rid of their intrusive images or thoughts. But the harder they try not to recall the trauma, the more they seem to think about it and the worse they feel. The treatment goal is not to seek to obliterate the intrusive imagery or thoughts but to contain them. Try placing an elastic band on your wrist and each time the intrusive image comes to mind, pull it and let it go. At the same time, tell yourself that you will watch a "mental video" of the trauma for twenty minutes at a certain time of the day. Or shout "Stop!" with plans to watch the video later. This generates a sense that you are in control of the images rather than them being in control of you. Be sure to set aside twenty minutes each day to do nothing but recall the abuse and think about it. If the appointed time comes each day for you to think about the abuse and you find it pointless, then postpone it until the next day's session.

2. Desensitization. When intrusion persists despite all efforts at containment, it may be useful to employ a desensitization procedure, but this strategy should not be used unless you have an established therapeutic alliance with a counselor or therapist. It is likely that this procedure will amplify your discomfort and distress before reducing it.

The desensitization procedure involves making a 10-15 minute audiotape of the original abuse trauma, describing the events that occurred in as much detail as possible, as well as the associated thoughts, feelings, and behaviors. Then you should play the tape at least once a day but not switch it off until you become more relaxed while listening to it. The particular aspects of the abusive events that cause you the most distress will often vary from day to day, as you view what happened from new and different angles as you try to make sense of it. You can practice a simple breathing procedure while listening to the tape: place a hand on your stomach, breathe in smoothly for a count of four, then out smoothly for a count of six, checking to make sure the stomach moves out on inhaling and in on exhaling.

Most victims do not like the idea of recording their trauma and listening to it. They have spent months, perhaps years, trying to avoid thinking about it! You need to understand that you are trading short-term pain for long-term relief.

An alternative to making a tape is for you to write about the abuse. Sit down in a quiet, private place where you will not be interrupted and write about what happened to you for half an hour a day for four consecutive days. Then take a two-day break. Repeat the procedure as long as needed. This activity can help you merge with the abusive experience, reevaluate it from different angles, and process it mentally as well as emotionally. The familiarity with the details of the abusive events over a few days can serve to diminish the intensity of your response to them. Don't just write about what happened. Also, describe how it made you feel at the time and how you feel about it now. Try expressing your feelings in poetry.

A third desensitization activity is to read about other people's abusive experiences, how they survived, and what they are doing to help themselves in recovery. Sharing other people's experiences may make your own a little less frightening and overwhelming. Studying child abuse—like you would math or English—will also help you gain a cognitive mastery over something that for most of your life has appeared incomprehensible. Gaining a cognitive mastery of the subject will make it easier to achieve a level of emotional stability in recalling it, diminishing the monster in your childhood to a bad experience in your adult memory.

3. Cognitive Restructuring. This is a process of accurately perceiving and recalling what happened and its effect upon you. Most victims tend to emphasize some details and minimize others. The treatment goal is for you to recall the whole picture of what happened, your responses, and its consequences—and not use a mental filter on the positive aspects. The goal is to reassess what happened, why it happened, and examine closely its effects upon you. A more realistic and accurate assessment of harm done will help alter your perception of having been damaged, ruined, or handicapped by the experiences. The perception of being wounded can be as distressing (and debilitating) as an actual wound.

4. Balancing Negative and Positive Memories. The purpose of this activity is not to ignore the negative aspects of the experience, nor negate the positive, but to strive to balance your memory of the experience with both positive and negative recollections. What did you say or do, for example, that may have protected a sibling or minimized the harm of your own experience or helped you survive?

Procedure: Identify specific thoughts or self-verbalizations related to the abuse that cause you distress. Then, with the help of a counselor, if needed, modify the negative self-verbalizations and replace them with positive self-statements. Replace, for example, the statement, "I'm so stupid! Why did I let him/her do it?" with, "I trusted him/her not to hurt me!"

By its very nature, abusive childhood experiences tend to be extremely graphic and vivid in your memory. Yet, many of us will acknowledge that there have been more good times in our lives than bad times. The problem is that the positive memories are less available and vivid, often overwhelmed by the intensity of the negative memories. The consequence is that the trauma memories assume an overwhelming importance in terms of our emotional state. Emotional health depends on a balance between positive and negative memories. The task of recovery is to recover those positive memories and use them to offset the negative memories.

Avoidance Reactions

Avoidance reactions generally take two primary forms: the first may involve an avoidance of situations that in some way remind you of the abusive experience, and the second is to try to escape from situations perceived as similar to the abuse. As well as behavioral avoidance, there is also cognitive avoidance—avoidance of thinking about the abuse or aspects of it. Avoidance behavior usually generalizes beyond the original context of abuse to include anything similar. The result is that your life becomes increasingly more constrained, isolated, and withdrawn. Your opportunities for achievement and pleasure are reduced—aggravating feelings of helplessness and victimization.

Three strategies are particularly useful in overcoming avoidance behavior: desensitization to avoided situations; cognitive restructuring—reassessing the degree of threat; and task orientation—using a problem-solving strategy.

1. Desensitization to Avoided Situations. It is common for survivors of child abuse to avoid situations that appear similar in some way to the original abusive situation when encountered unexpectedly.

The starting point for the desensitization procedure is to specifically identify those situations that now pose a threat to you. Rank the situations in terms of how important they are to you, the amount of effort you make to avoid them, and the level of discomfort they cause you. Then, construct a ladder with the most difficult task at the top rung of the ladder and the least difficult at the bottom rung, with other tasks arranged in order of anticipated difficulty on the rungs between. Recovery will involve starting at the bottom rung, trying to accomplish each task, and climbing the ladder. Add additional ministeps between each rung, if needed. The goal is to test the safety of avoided situations through a series of miniexperiments involving gradual exposure to the situation.

2. Cognitive Restructuring (reassessing the degree of threat). Child abuse raises serious questions in the minds of victims about the dangerousness of the world, the trustworthiness of people, about their own continued safety and their ability to take care of themselves and survive. The answers to these questions have an important influence on your emotional state and behavior. The procedure is to set up experimental tests designed to confirm or deny your irrational beliefs. It is important that you view your negative beliefs as hypotheses to be tested rather than as facts to be submitted to. Here are some of the questions you need to answer:

    a. Is the world benevolent or malevolent?

    b. Is life meaningful or meaningless?

    c. Am I worthy or unworthy?

    d. Are people trustworthy or untrustworthy?

    e. Is the world predictable or unpredictable?

    f. Am I capable of taking care of myself or am I helpless?

    g. Can I have what I want most in life, or am I doomed?

    h. Am I attractive enough to attract intimacy, or will I be alone and estranged forever?

    i. Do I have a place in the scheme of things, or am I just an accident that should never have happened?

    j. Do I have a future that I can control, or do I have to live one day at a time trying to survive?

FROM VICTIM TO VICTORY

It is important to focus on the current environment and assess realistically the degree of threat posed by it. Your appraisal of the environment can be affected by faulty beliefs such as:[3]

- **All-or-nothing Thinking:** Everything is seen in black-and-white terms; for example, "I am either in control of what's happening to me or I'm not."

- **Overgeneralization:** Expecting a uniform response from a category of people because of the misdeeds of a member; for example, "All men are potential rapists."

- **Mental Filter:** Seizing on a negative fragment of a situation and dwelling on it; for example, "I could have been killed in that encounter!"

- **Automatic Discounting:** Brushing aside the positive aspects of what was achieved in a traumatic situation; like "I was only doing what I was supposed to when I saved my sister's life."

- **Jumping to Conclusions:** Assuming that it is known what others think; for example, "They all think I should just forget it and go on with my life."

- **Magnification and Minimization:** Magnification of shortcomings and minimization of strengths; for example, "Since the abuse I can't seem to do anything right and can just barely keep my grades up in school!"

- **Emotional Reasoning:** Focusing on an emotional state to draw conclusions about oneself; for example, "Since it happened, I'm frightened of my own shadow; I guess I'm just a wimp."

- **Should Statements:** Inappropriate use of moral imperatives, shoulds, musts, have tos, oughts (e.g., "It's ridiculous that I can't be in the same room alone with him now. I should be able to forgive and forget!")

- **Labeling and Mislabeling:** The inappropriate use of characterizations to describe oneself or others; for example, "I used to think that I was a good kid. But since the abuse, I wonder if there isn't something wrong with me."

- **Personalization:** Assuming that because something bad happened or went wrong, it must be your fault; for example, "What did I do to provoke him? I must have said or done something to make him so mad."

It is important that you identify and challenge your faulty beliefs. People tend to behave in ways that are consistent with their value/belief systems. If those systems are faulty, the result may be inappropriate or self-defeating behaviors. Faulty beliefs must be challenged at two levels: first, whether they are actually true or not, and second, whether they accomplish for you what you want in your life. Faulty beliefs can result in impaired thinking, such as the following:

- *"I'm a dummy":* Thoughts focus on worthlessness, low self-esteem, inadequacy, incompetence, and helplessness. Feeling defeated, the attitude is one of "what's the use of trying?" Shows a lack of self-confidence. "I'm too dumb to get it right!" or "I just can't keep up!" or "I never do anything right, so why bother?"

- *"I'll show you!":* Thoughts focus on anger, outrage, hostility, and revenge. Anger becomes the central theme that affects all other thinking. Raging can become a tool for manipulation. "They have no right to treat me this way!" or "I'll get even with them!"

- *"I'm the one and only":* Thoughts focus on excessive pride, ego, narcissism (total focus on self), conceit, vanity, being self-centered. These thoughts provoke feelings of being unique, special, atypical, different, better than others. "I'm smart enough to get whatever I want!" or "You can never understand me!" or "Those rules don't apply to me!"

- *"It's my way or no way!":* Thoughts focus on being in control, overpowering others, demanding from others, commanding others to do what is wanted. They tend to measure their self-worth by the amount of control they have over others in every situation. "I can talk them into anything!" or "I should be the leader!" or "I can do it better than anyone else!"

- *"There're only two ways—my way and the wrong way!":* Thoughts focus on dividing the world into two distinct, different, and often opposite sides. Everything is polarized, either one way or another. Tend to think in absolutes, all or nothing, right or wrong with no gray areas. "Women are out to get what they can from men!" or "All a man wants is sex!" or "Children are selfish!"

131

- *"I'm an airhead!"*: Thinking is confused, involving a series of scattered and fragmented pieces, usually to cover up, divert attention from, or to avoid unpleasant situations. Person is unable to stay on track in a conversation.

- *"I expect nothing but the best!"* Thinking is focused on unrealistic expectations, unrealistic optimism, grandiose ideas of what is possible, or what will happen. "I can plan the perfect crime!" or "I'll make a million on this deal!" or "I'll never get caught!"

- *"I live in trash city!"*: Thinking is focused on everything negative about life and people. Everything is bad, can't see potential good or anything positive about people, events, or life situations. "Life sucks!" or "I can't trust anybody!" or "Wait for the other shoe to drop before you start celebrating!"

- *"What they don't know won't hurt them!"* Thoughts are focused on not letting anyone know what you are thinking, feeling, or doing. This includes all dishonesty, big lies and little ones, including avoiding the truth. "I wasn't doing anything!" or "I walked by her room, but I didn't look in!"

- *"It's me against the world!"*: Thinking is focused on fear, constant suspicion, thinking that others are out to get you, ridicule you, hurt, humiliate, or betray you, or put you down. People cannot be trusted. "They'll make fun of me if I show my feelings!" or "They're trying to set me up!" or "They're out to get me!"

- *"I'm right and you're wrong!"*: Thoughts narrow down to one main idea, one track, or one side of an issue, blocking out everything else. They become single-minded, closed to suggestions or other ideas, locked onto a single thought or perspective. They tend to be inflexible, unresponsive, and fanatical. "You don't know what you're talking about!" or "You can talk all you want, but you won't change my mind!"

- *"People are just like me—no better, no worse!"*: This involves projecting your own thoughts, feelings, behaviors, motivations, beliefs, faults, and so forth, upon others. For example, a person who lies might conclude that everybody lies and cannot be trusted to tell the truth. "If it's true of me, it's true of you!"

- *"You hurt me!"*: Victimized thinking, focused on seeing the world as an unjust, unfair, dangerous place. They tend to turn circumstances around in order to show themselves as the victim, the target, the underdog, and to interpret life events and what is said in such a way as to appear the victim. There can be great power in being a victim. "People are prejudiced!" or "The world is unfair!"

- *"Yeah, I'm bad!":* Thoughts focus on being belligerent, hostile, aggressive, and rude. They tend to be discourteous, contemptuous, and disrespectful of other people. "People are no better than I am, and that's not much!"

- *"Hey, it's not my fault!":* This is irresponsible thinking where persons refuse to assume responsibility for anything bad that happens in their lives or as a result of their action or inaction. "It's not my fault that nothing seems to go right for us!"

- *"Aw, it's not so bad!":* This is avoidance thinking that pretends that things aren't as bad as they are, which denies the truth, often to themselves as well as to others. Denial is a way to avoid painful, uncomfortable, and conflictual situations. "Everything will be OK if we just leave it alone!" or "Just because I don't feel good does not mean I have a hangover!"

- *"Yes, you started it!":* This thinking is focused upon pushing responsibility onto others, blaming them for one's own misfortunes, mistakes, and misadventures, such as, "It wasn't my idea!" or "You said it first!"

- *"What's mine is mine—and I deserve it!":* This is a false sense of ownership, a feeling of being entitled, as if it is owed or due to the person. Ownership (possession) brings privileges. "It's my kid; I can do what I want with him!" or "I bought her dinner, so she owes me sex!"

- *"I'm a worrywart!":* Thinking is rooted in anxiety, focusing on fear, dread, doom, and distress. They tend to believe Murphy's Law that if something can go wrong, it will. "Something bad is going to happen—I just know it!"

- *"I can't make it without you, Baby!":* Thinking that asserts that the person cannot function alone, can't do anything themselves, must rely on others for things they could do themselves. Being overdependent. "I can't go through this by myself!" or "I can't do this alone!"

- *"Hey, whatever works!"*: This is being superficial, insincere, running a con to get what is wanted. Manipulating people by saying or doing what is expected for an ulterior motive. "She won't get mad if I can come up with the right excuse!"

- *"Later, man!"*: This is the procrastinator who avoids assuming responsibility for his action or inaction by putting things off to another day. Never do today what you can do tomorrow. "I'll think about that later!"

- *"So tell someone who cares!"*: This is an attitude of indifference, apathy, detachment, an aloofness suggesting that nothing is important to me and I am invulnerable. "So what?" or "Who cares what they think?"

- *"Whatever you say is OK with me!"*: This is being passive and unassertive. Giving in, going along with another's plans, wants, desires, or wishes, even when they conflict with their own. This involves appeasing others even if they don't want to be appeased. "You decide" or "I don't care what we do" or "You're the boss!"

- *"So, what's the big deal?"*: This is thinking which minimizes, belittles, or diminshes the significance or importance of a behavior, event, achievement, want, and its impact on oneself and others. "She'll get over it; it wasn't that bad!"

Each of these examples of impaired thinking arises out of a faulty belief about yourself, others, or the world around you, and each is accompanied by its own set of emotions and special way of acting out those feelings behaviorally. Changing feelings and behavior begins by identifying, correcting, or replacing faulty beliefs and impaired thinking with beliefs that will stimulate the kind of thinking that will achieve for you what you want out of life.

3. Task Orientation. Survivors of child abuse not only tend to avoid threatening situations, but they also may disengage from meaningful and purposeful activity, like school hobbies, church, and even relationships. Task orientation is a strategy designed to get you once again engaged in daily activities important to you. The goal is to get your attention off of self-evaluation involving a "how do I feel today?" focus to instead a "what can I do to help myself today?" focus. It is a strategy that involves identifying and solving problems. *Procedure:* Identify the most pressing problems facing you today. The hardest part of solving any problem is first defining the problem. Be specific. Then prioritize the problems in terms of which is most important to you and most urgent. Then, taking the most pressing problem first, apply the following problem-solving strategy:

a. Define the problem as specifically as possible.

b. Brainstorm as many possible solutions as you can imagine.

c. Evaluate all the solutions, rating them in terms of feasibility and possibility. Be realistic.

d. Eliminate all those which are "impossible," "improbable," and "not worth the effort."

e. Evaluate the advantages and disadvantages of each remaining solution. Consider costs in terms of time, energy, and money.

f. Choose a solution.

g. Develop a step-by-step plan of action for achieving the solution.

h. Gather whatever resources are needed, if any.

i. Then ACT! Put your plan into action.

j. Periodically review the outcome of your solution, making adjustments as needed.

Most survivors of child abuse grow into adults believing that they have limited choices, opportunities, and means to achieve what they want in life. They often feel frustrated, powerless, and defeated. Recovery requires you to acquire the knowledge and skills necessary to achieve your goals or that you clarify and redefine your goals so that they are achievable. This problem-solving strategy is a good place to start.

Heightened Arousal

It is not uncommon for survivors of child abuse to experience hypersensitivity and hyperreactivity when they feel threatened by their memories of abuse. The results are often feelings of anxiety, nervousness, and restlessness. These symptoms are often expressed through hyperactivity, hypervigilance, and hypercriticalness. The following stress management activities are most effective in relieving these symptoms:

1. Exercise. Exercise, like humor, is one of the guardians of

135

mental and emotional health. It is virtually impossible to be depressed, for example, when you are exercising. The brain releases endorphines during exercise—the same hormone that is released during love making—which bring a sense of euphoria and well being. It also enhances the immune system by stimulating the production of white blood cells, the cells that fight sickness and disease.

Physical exertion gives a physical and tangible outlet for strong emotions. In every instance of heightened arousal, we have three options about how to deal with them: first, we can act them out destructively, harming ourselves or others; we can act them out constructively, sparing ourselves and others, or we can sit still and boil in our emotional juices! Exercising is acting out constructively. There is tremendous therapeutic value in physical activity like walking, dancing, jogging, swimming, or aerobics. Not only does it help relieve emotional pressure, but it also shapes the body and refreshes the spirit!

2. Talk. Talking it out is another effective stress management skill. The verbal release of pent-up emotion can be very therapeutic. But it is important to find someone you can trust, who will not take what you say or how you say it personally and will listen without trying to "correct" your thinking or "alter" your feelings. Peace of mind comes when we speak the truth and are authentic privately as well as publicly. You are who you are, and you feel the way you feel. Recovery requires that you accept yourself as you are and allow others to do the same.

3. Expression Through Art. The important thing is that you not keep the feelings bottled up within you. Find a way to express them—to allow them to flow freely out of you. Write it out on paper, paint it on canvas, motion it in dance, or shape it in clay. Find what works best for you; then practice it regularly. Strong emotions are like storms: frightening in their coming but refreshing in their passing. Not only will you find relief in the expression of feelings through art, but you may also end up writing a book or painting a picture!

4. Diet. What you eat and drink has a lot to do with how you feel and cope with stress. Consuming stimulants, like sodas, for example, when you feel nervous and restless will likely only make the feelings worse. Trying to "comfort" yourself with a cigarette when you feel scared or lonely will likely make you only feel more depressed. Consult your physician for healthy diet recommendations if you are not sure. Controlling your diet will not only give you a sense of control over what goes into your body, but will also start the process of "body imaging." This is where you imagine how you want your body to look and then begin working to sculpt and shape it into that image.

5. Humor. Few activities are as cathartic and relieving as is humor. It is a second pillar of mental health. Being able to see the humor in life, ourselves, and others means that we are not taking them too seriously. To laugh requires that we "turn loose" of the control we have on our emotions, to allow them to flow naturally and spontaneously. A good laugh is like water pouring through a ruptured dam: it continues until it has all run out. Surround yourself with humorous artifacts, articles, movies, music, and people. There are some things in life that we simply cannot control or change. We can either cry about it or laugh at it. Whereas crying can hold us in bondage to what we cannot control, laughing at it frees us so that we do not suffer because of it. Set aside a period of time each day for entertainment, when your primary goal is to laugh!

6. Breathing and Relaxation Exercises. A state of heightened arousal is characterized by confused thinking, rapid heartbeat, and shallow respiration. There is great therapeutic value in stopping whatever you are doing, right where you are, to focus your mind on something comforting or soothing, relaxing your body by tensing your muscles and then releasing them, and by taking deep breaths, holding them, and then releasing them. There are many breathing and relaxation exercises that you can try until you find the ones most effective for you. Perhaps a trip to the local library in search of these techniques would be a good way to take control of this part of your recovery.

7. Affirmations. The human brain is much like a computer. It consists of what we can see on the monitor and can control through editing and design. But it also consists of what we cannot see, the "hidden" programming that actually "runs" the programs that make the computer useful to us. Without that hidden programming, computers would not work. But if programmed properly, computers can do many wonderful and marvelous things to make life easier and more pleasant for us.

Similarly, the human brain has the "conscious mind" which contains the mental screen upon which we can see images, receive sensory input, process thinking, and create new ideas. It is this part of the mind over which we have direct control. But like the computer, there is also a "hidden" part of the mind, the subconscious, which contains all the information and data needed to make what happens in the conscious mind possible. Most of what happens in the conscious mind depends upon what is programmed into the subconscious mind, for it is here that we store our values and beliefs, the "data" and "facts" we believe to be true about all persons and things. Unfortunately, the subconscious mind does not test or evaluate the truth or reliability of what the conscious mind tells it. It merely accepts it as fact and stores it for future use.

The subconscious minds of abused children have been programmed with negative, inaccurate data—lies, half-truths, and illusions. These buried, subconscious, faulty beliefs are what the conscious mind uses to interpret reality.

Part of recovery involves a process of reprogramming the subconscious mind with positive data, values, and beliefs which more accurately reflect reality. One of the most effective ways to do this is through the use of affirmations. Affirmations are simply positive statements that are repeated over and over in our conscious mind until the subconscious mind accepts them as fact and uses them to replace the negative thoughts put there during childhood. These affirmations need to be repeated several times a day, especially during times of relaxation. Some important affirmations might include:

a. I am me, all that I should be, whole and complete.

b. I am a good person, worthy of love and respect.

c. I am in control of my life, my thoughts, feelings, and behavior.

d. Life is good to me, and I am glad to be alive.

e. Every day and in every way, I am getting better and better, healthier and healthier, happier and happier.

Make up your own affirmations. State them as if they are already true. It doesn't matter whether you believe them at this point. Your subconscious mind will accept them as truth and work to fulfill them in your life.

8. Visualization. There is an old adage that says, "If you can imagine it, you can do it!" The human brain has an incredible creative power to bring into reality what it imagines as possibility. Every new invention, creation, notion, and expression was first conceived in the mind. The power of the brain to find solutions to problems, bring about personality changes, and facilitate healing is well known by many who work with traumatized people. Apart from faith, nothing has more power than our imagination to help us make our life into what we want it to be. I have witnessed the power of visualization to bring about desired changes not only in my own life, but in the lives of others as well, including that of my own son.

On the eve of entering high school, my son came to me in consternation.

"Papa," he said, "I don't want to be a lineman anymore!"

"Does that mean you don't want to play football anymore?" I asked.

"No. I just don't want to be a lineman. I'm tired of getting beat up on every play!" he explained.

"Well, what position would you like to play?" I asked.

"I want to be a quarterback!" he answered wtihout hesitation. It was apparent to me that he had thought a lot about this already.

"Then why don't you try out for quarterback?"

"Because everybody will laugh at me!" he moaned.

"Son, there are two kinds of people in the world," I told him. "There are those who know what they want and are willing to take the risks involved in getting it, like having people laugh at them, and possibly achieving what they want in life. Then there are those who are uncertain about what they want and are too afraid of what other people might think, so they don't evey try. You will never get what you want in life unless you are willing to go after it. You need to decide what kind of person you're going to be."

"But I don't know how to be a quarterback!" he complained further.

He was right. He had never taken a snap from center, carried the ball, or thrown a pass in a football game. Because of his size, his experience on the football field was limited to being a lineman.

"If you really want to be a quarterback, here's what you can do," I advised. "Go up to the coach at the first practice and tell him you want to try out for quarterback. Everybody will laugh at you, but that's OK because the coach will give you your chance to try out.

And that's the first step to becoming what you want to be. So when he sends you over to the quarterbacks, get in the back of the line and watch closely what the other quarterbacks are doing. Then in your mind, imagine yourself doing the same thing over and over again. But as you see yourself doing it in your mind, imagine doing it just a little bit smoother and quicker than the others."

My son answered that he would think about it. Nothing more was said until he came home after the first day of school and football practice.

"Papa, I decided you're right," he said to me as I was starting supper in the kitchen. "I want to be the kind of person who knows what they want and goes after it."

"Does that mean you tried out for quarterback today?" I asked.

"Yes," he answered. "I did just like you suggested. I went right up to the coach in front of the whole team and told him I wanted to try out for quarterback. Everybody laughed at me, but he sent me over to the quarterbacks, like you said he would. I got in the back of the line and watched what the others were doing, and then imagined myself doing it."

"So, how did it go?"

"I guess I did OK," he answered with a huge smile. "The coach wants me back with the quarterbacks tomorrow!"

By the time the season started, this kid, who had never thrown a pass or carried the ball in a football game, beat out all the experienced quarterbacks and led the freshman team to an undefeated city championship! Today he is a college quarterback on full scholarship, standing on the threshold of a possible National Football League career.

He was able to achieve what he wanted because he could envision himself being a quarterback, practiced being a quarterback in his mind first, was willing to take the risks involved with going after what he wanted, and was willing to be last in line so that he could learn from others.

In my own experience, as late as 1982, a professor I admired and respected in my doctoral program advised me that I would never be a writer because I did not have the necessary language and writing skills. My first book was published two years later!

There will always be doubters and detracters, people who will tell us that whatever we want to do is impossible or unreasonable or unachievable. We cannot allow ourselves to be limited by the uncertainties and cynicism of others.

Visualization involves vividly and clearly "picturing" in your mind what you want, truly believing that it is achievable, wanting it enough to take the risks involved in attaining it, and then enthusiastically and faithfully acting to bring it about. If we can imagine it, we can do it!

9. Healthy Risk Taking. Being alive means confronting risks in many ways every day. The risk of standing up is that we may fall down. The risk of driving a car is that we may be involved in an accident. In living, we risk unexpected death. But if we never stand up, we'll never walk. Similarly, if we never drive a car, it will be difficult for us to get where we want to go. And what would life be like if we lived each moment in constant fear of dying?

Recovery requires that we take the risks necessary to bring about healing—the risk of confronting the truth, of trusting others—to believe in ourselves, knowing that we have the power and tools within us to make life what we want it to be. Recovery means releasing our fear so that we can firmly grasp the opportunities for growth and change which come to us each day.

Healthy risks are those with a minimum chance of failure and disappointment, and a maximum chance of success and fulfillment. Assessing risks is a skill you may have to learn with the help of a trained counselor. It has been said that a journey of a thousand miles begins with the first step. If the first step is never taken, there never will be a last step. Recovery means taking that first step, and then another, and another, until at last we are headed toward where we want to go. Recovery is a lifelong journey into wholeness, to reclaim the self and find peace.

10. Prayer and Meditation. Through prayer and meditation we "connect" at a deep spiritual level with the source of all life, all love, and all healing. To pray and meditate, we must turn loose of everything external to us, to disengage from worldly concerns, and free ourselves from human pettiness to turn inward, to come face to face with our most authentic self as we stand in the presence of God. Being scrutinized by God, standing humbly before God, and feeling the warmth of God's enveloping love, casts a new light on what is and is not important in our life!

There was a song called "The Touch of the Master's Hand," sung some years ago by country musician Bill Anderson. The song tells of an old, worn, and battered violin being auctioned off to the highest bidder. No one would bid more than a dollar or two for the relic of what must have once been a fine musical instrument worth hundreds of dollars. Suddenly an old man in the back of the room came forward and gently took the violin into his hands, tightened its strings, and began to play. The music produced at his hand was beautiful and enchanting, moving many to appreciate the violin for what it really was, rather than just for what it appeared to be. The bidding was renewed and grew to several thousand dollars before the violin was sold. It was the touch of the master's hand that made all the difference.

So, too, like the violin, it is the touch of the Master's hand in our life that gives it meaning and value. Like the sculptor shaping his clay, it is the touch of the Master's hand that shapes us into the masterpiece—the miracle—that we are, valued by the Creator above all things. It is in prayer that we find our true value, for it is there, as we stand in the presence of God, that we are most truly who we are, bruised and fractured perhaps, but authentically ourselves. It is there in God's loving acceptance that we recover what has been lost—and become whole, fulfilled, and complete.

CONCLUSION

For many of us, the most damaging effect of child abuse is that it leaves us in bondage—bondage to shame, to self-defeating thinking and behavior, to uncontrollable emotions and painful, merciless memories of abuse—in bondage to a past that is a prison no less real than those with stone walls and bars. We are never truly "recovered" until we are freed from that bondage.

To be in bondage is to be held in debt to someone or something, usually against our wills. It typically requires payment of the debt to free us from the bondage. The bondage of sin, for example, is guilt and shame. Punishment for sins often brings release from the guilt and shame—because we have paid for our misdeeds.

But there is a reverse kind of bondage as well. It occurs when others owe us. When we are wronged, the offender owes us an apology and restitution. By harboring resentment, we bind them to us at some level until the debt is paid.

Victims of child abuse have been wronged. A crime has been committed against us. Something has been lost in the experience that cannot be reclaimed, and we may be permanently scarred and affected by the abuse. By all rights, the abuser owes the victim an explanation, an apology, and reparations for the harm done. The abuser needs to be held legally and emotionally accountable until the debt is paid.

The problem for most survivors is this: our bodies can heal in time given proper medical attention and care. Our minds and faulty beliefs can heal given proper psychotherapy. Emotionally we can heal by expressing and dealing with our feelings about what happened to us. But so long as we are owed a debt by the abuser, we cannot heal spiritually. We must continue to hold the account open, maintain a running total of what is owed, continue to resent the unresponsiveness of the debtor, invest valuable time and energy in trying to collect the debt, and all the while being reminded of the injustice of our victimization. We live our lives waiting for the abuser to admit his crime, assume responsibility for it, apologize to us, and then make reparations to us for the harm they have done. In essence, we surrender control of our life to the abuser, putting everything on hold as we wait for him to do the right thing! We are held hostage emotionally and spiritually by the very person who owes us the debt, the very person we probably dislike the most—our abuser! In the meantime, the poisons of repressed anger and resentment eat away at us, spilling over into other relationships important to us. We may stagnate in our growth and development, and we may act out the unresolved hostility within us by doing things that threaten our health and well-being further, things that are self-destructive. Instead of punishing the abuser, we end up punishing ourselves by not resolving the issue.

The final step in the recovery process, the key that will unlock the prison door of our pasts, the action that will free us from bondage at last, is the act of forgiveness. We must forgive the abuser. This does not mean forget the abuse, erase it as if it never happened, rescue the abuser from the consequences of his actions, nor does it mean to condone, sanction, excuse, or ignore what was done to us. To "forgive" means to "cancel a debt." It means to forget our need for a confession, an apology, revenge, and reparations. Nothing in the world can change what was done to us. The only thing we have the power to change is what we will do with ourselves and others today, tomorrow, and in the days ahead. There is no doubt that the abuser owes us these things. But we owe it to ourselves to go on and live our lives without them, to not wait around wanting, needing, expecting restitution that may never come. Our reward for surviving is the rest of our lives! But it can be truly ours only when no one else has a claim on it. By canceling the abuser's debt, we will have no other connection to that person, and we will be free then to pursue our lives as we please. Healing can occur only when we let go of what is hurting us. Only through forgiveness—canceling the debt owed to us—can we know the true meaning of freedom and fully recover what was lost.

Victory comes to those who can end the war, resolve the conflict, and begin a new life, at peace with themselves, with others, with the world, and with God. *Tempus praeteritum resolve et carpe diem!*

The Oliver Twist
Syndrome

Some children seem to be able to survive better and recover quicker from the stress and hazards of abuse than others. Some contributing factors include:

1. **Rapid Response to Danger.** The ability to recognize and adapt to the requirements of the immediate situation of threat in order to avoid or minimize harm (e.g., silence, hiding, compliance, performing a task).
2. **Precocious or Pseudomature Behavior.** The ability to look, sound, and behave less like a child and more like an adult in threatening situations (e.g., role reversal, assuming adult responsibilities, controlling own emotions, denying own wants and needs and desires).
3. **Disassociation of Affect.** The ability to distance oneself from own intense feelings (e.g., selective forgetting, blocking pain, denial).
4. **Formation of Survival Relationships.** The ability to establish relationships that will result in critical help and support during times of crisis (e.g., with teacher, coach, peer, pastor, adults in other families).
5. **Positive Projective Anticipation.** The ability to project oneself into the future and fantasize about how life will be better and different when the difficult times are over.
6. **Decisive Risk Taking.** The ability to make crucial decisions and deal with their consequences in the midst of threat while

maintaining a sense of autonomy and identity apart from the offender.

7. **The Conviction of Being Loved.** The ability to continue believing they are loved despite negative life circumstances. Requires that the children have enough self-esteem to believe they are worthy of love.

8. **Cognitive Restructuring of Painful Experiences.** The ability to process past negative events in one's own mind in order to make them more acceptable and congruent with own current view of life and reality, and to reassess their ultimate effects.

9. **Altruism.** The ability to get pleasure and satisfaction from giving to others what one would like to receive oneself.

10. **Optimism and Hope.** The ability to maintain a life orientation that looks forward to a positive future. Person is controlled and motivated more by what is going to happen than by what has already happened.

11. **Externalization of Symptomology.** The ability to express authentic emotion at the time of the abuse, rather than internalizing it. Feeling safe enough to express feelings to someone and have them validated.

12. **Active Resisting.** The ability to make an effort to protect oneself from the abuse (e.g., refusing to accept responsibility for the abuse, running away, hiding, avoidance, telling the perpetrator to stop, acting out to attract attention).

Early Childhood Maladaptive Beliefs and Their Consequent Emotional Dilemmas

Autonomy

1. **Dependence.** The belief that you are unable to function successfully on your own and so you need the constant support and help of others. Your welfare depends on the good will of others. Psychological dilemma: survival demands that you acknowledge and accept your dependence on others (e.g., parents for food, shelter, protection) while at the same time finding ways to survive without them due to abuse or neglect.

2. **Subjugation or Lack of Individuation.** The belief that survival depends on pleasing others, requiring that others' wants and needs must always come first. Involves the voluntary or involuntary sacrifice of your own needs to satisfy the needs of others with an accompanying failure to recognize your own needs. Psychological dilemma: survival demands that you take care of others while at the same time taking care of yourself.

3. **Vulnerability to Harm or Illness.** The fear that disaster is about to strike at any time (natural, interpersonal, criminal, medical, or financial). Survival demands that you expect and be prepared for the worst at all times. Psychological dilemma: survival requires that you acknowledge your vulnerabilities while at the same time overcoming them.

4. **Fear of Losing Self-control.** The fear that you will involuntarily lose control of your own behavior, impulses, emotions, thoughts, body, and so on. Psychological dilemma: survival demands staying in control at all times while at the same time trusting others in authority not to hurt you in the provision of basic life needs, protection, education, health care, and so on.

5. **Genetic Predisposition.** The fear of becoming like another due to genetic ties, same sex, or biological similarities, especially parents. Psychological dilemma: survival demands accepting your family while overcoming your "bad seed, bad blood, or bad breeding."

6. **Ecological Entrapment.** The belief that ecological factors (where you live, how much money you have, race) are beyond your control and dictate the quality of your life. Psychological dilemma: survival demands living within, yet overcoming real or perceived ecological constraints.

Connectedness

7. **Emotional Deprivation.** The expectation that your needs for nurturance, empathy, affection, and caring will never be adequately met by others. Psychological dilemma: survival demands that you live in a relationship to meet basic needs while at the same time not becoming dependent or vulnerable to them.

8. **Abandonment or Loss.** Fear that you will imminently lose significant others and be emotionally isolated forever. Based on the belief that something is fundamentally wrong with you that makes you unworthy of love, and thereby unacceptable to others. Psychological dilemma: survival demands engagement with others while at the same time you remain detached and independent.

9. **Mistrust.** The expectation that others will willfully hurt, abuse, cheat, lie, manipulate, or take advantage of you. Based on the belief that people and the world are basically selfish, malevolent, untrustworthy, and unsafe. Psychological dilemma: sur-

vival requires intimacy with others while at the same time not being intimate enough that they can hurt you.

10. **Social Isolation or Alienation.** The feeling that you are isolated from the rest of the world, different from other people, or not a part of any group or community. Based on the belief that "if people really knew me they . . ." would not like, accept, love me. Psychological dilemma: survival requires living and working with others while at the same time not getting close enough to them that they get to know the real you with all your flaws and inadequacies.

Worthiness

11. **Defectiveness or Unlovability.** The feeling that you are inwardly defective and flawed or that you are unlovable. Based on the belief that bad things happen to bad people. Psychological dilemma: survival demands being aware of your defectiveness so as not to expect too much while at the same time being able and competent.

12. **Social Undesirability.** The belief that one is outwardly undesirable or unattractive to others (e.g., ugly, sexually undesirable, low in status, poor conversational skills, dull, boring, unimportant). Derives from the belief that others determine your value. Psychological dilemma: survival demands that you relate to others while at the same time expecting to be rejected.

13. **Incompetence or Failure.** The belief that you cannot perform competently in areas of achievement (school, activity, sport, or career), daily responsibilities to self and others, or decision making. Psychological dilemma: survival requires that you remain a victim and not risk further failure while at the same time performing at survival levels.

14. **Guilt or Punishment.** The belief that you are morally or ethically bad or irresponsible and deserving of harsh criticism or punishment. Derives from the belief that bad things are punishment for bad people and that somehow abuse victims deserve their abuse. Psychological dilemma: survival demands that

pleasure be derived from life and relationships while at the same time making sure that you are punished for being bad so that others will not have to inflict the punishment.

15. **Shame or Embarrassment.** Recurrent feelings of shame or self-consciousness experienced because you believe that your inadequacies are totally unacceptable to others and are constantly exposed. Psychological dilemma: survival demands that you remain self-conscious while at the same time being other-conscious.

Limits and Standards

16. **Unrelenting Standards.** The relentless striving to meet extremely high expectations of yourself at the expense of happiness, pleasure, health, sense of accomplishment, or satisfying relationships. Psychological dilemma: survival demands that you be perfect and flawless while at the same time accepting your limitations and humanity.

17. **Entitlement or Insufficient Limits.** Insistence that you be able to do, say, or have whatever you want immediately. Involves disregard for: what others consider reasonable, what is actually feasible, the time or patience usually required or the cost to others, or difficulty with self-discipline. Based on the belief that the rules are suspended because you live in a suspended reality controlled by another. Psychological dilemma: survival demands that you live within the laws and limits while at the same time finding ways to meet those needs denied by the limitations imposed upon you.

Meaning and Purpose

18. **Fatalism.** The belief that life is fate and that destiny controls life events; that it "was meant to be." Persistent feelings of helplessness to effect change and a hopelessness that things will get better. Psychological dilemma: survival demands that you take charge and initiate change while at the same time acknowledging that your life is controlled mostly by chance and luck (e.g., being in the wrong place at the wrong time).

19. **Chaos.** The belief that life is unpredictable and therefore unmanageable. It is irrational and does not make sense. Survival requires an aggressive response to ever-changing life situations.

    Psychological Dilemma: Survival requires not asking too many questions, while at the same time seeking answers, in hope of preventing a recurrence of the trauma.

20. **Aimlessness.** The belief that life has no purpose beyond self-gratification. The quality of life is dictated by one's responsiveness to life's demands. If you don't know where you're going, any road will do. Psychological dilemma: survival requires that you be ready to "go with the flow," while at the same time being ready to go "against the flow" to get where you want to go.

21. **Existential Relativism.** There is no meaning beyond the present moment. Reality is relative to perceptions and individual interpretations. Psychological dilemma: survival requires that you live "in the world" but not be "of the world," that you live among others while living without them.

22. **Survivalist.** The belief that the goal of life is to survive. Life is what you do while you are waiting to die. Psychological dilemma: survival demands that you avoid pain while at the same time heal and recover from it.

Understanding
Children's Behavior

There are three basic sets of behaviors used to cope with life and its endless, challenging demands when children feel powerless and out of control:

I. **Defensive Aggressive Behaviors** (aggressive behaviors designed to protect, defend, and shield oneself from harm)
   A. Acting out
      1. Violence
         a. physical and verbal assault
         b. defiance—quiet aggression
         c. destructiveness—often used to punish others for a perceived wrong
         d. fighting
      2. Stealing—physically lashing out without hurting anyone physically
      3. Obscenity
      4. Name calling
      5. Compulsive talking
      6. Habitual lying
      7. Vandalism—destruction of property is a cry for help. Destruction of a loved object is the loudest cry because it represents destruction of the self.
   B. Self-destructive behaviors
      1. Suicide—the ultimate self-destruction, resulting from a perceived eternal, changeless misery

2. Psychosomatic illnesses
   a. headaches
   b. stomachaches
      (1) vomiting
      (2) constipation
      (3) diarrhea
      (4) nausea
   c. asthma—being smothered
   d. eczema—constant, unrelieved irritation
   e. ulcers—being eaten up
   f. mouth problems
      (1) canker sores
      (2) trench mouth
      (3) bruxism (grinding teeth)
      (4) cheek and lip biting
      (5) split gums
   g. anorexia
   h. bulimia
   i. accidents
   j. high risk taking
   k. self-mutilation
   l. ingesting poisons
      (1) drugs
      (2) alcohol
      (3) smoking
   m. suicide gestures

II. **Escape Behaviors**
   A. Denying reality—a fugitive from life.
   B. Make it go away—close eyes, ears, mind—deny that there is anything wrong.
   C. Withdraw behind emotional wall.
   D. Procrastination—postpone the unpleasant.
   E. Forgetting—eliminate the unpleasant.
   F. Channel into something else—like music or writing.
   G. Daydreaming—playing games to avoid dealing with it or idealizing the situation.
   H. Development of fears and phobias
   I. Make self go away:
      1. Sleep

2. Television
3. Immersion in studies or activities
4. Play acting as someone else
5. Daydreaming
6. Running away

J. Drugs and alcohol
K. Sex—escape of the lonely ("getting love"). Also a way to escape failures and inadequacies.
L. Illness—escape responsibilities and accountability.

III. Apathy

A. A retreat from feelings.
B. Settling for safety rather than taking risks.
C. Survival through no feelings at all.
D. Commitment means caring.
E. There is safety in detachment.
F. Fear of vulnerability.
G. Severed communication—there is no link to the outside world.
H. Remain the center of their own universe, unfulfilled, cut off, listless, and bored.
I. Children lose touch with the world around them when they are forbidden to touch or explore it—loss of excitement and stimulation.
J. Sense of failure—in the unbearable pain of their failure to win love, they stop loving.
K. Apathy is as lethal as murder or suicide. Children who turn to apathy as a means of coping with their hurts are as tragic as victims of death. Perhaps more tragic, for their attempts to cope are the height of irony: they make themselves dead in order to live.

APPENDIX 4

What Is Child Abuse?

Child Abuse—Serious physical or mental injury that is not explained by the available medical history as being accidental, or sexual abuse or sexual exploitation, or serious physical neglect of a child under eighteen years of age; if the injury, abuse, or neglect has been caused by the acts or omissions of the child's parents or by a person responsible for the child's welfare, or any individual residing in the same home as the child or a paramour of a child's parents, provided, however, that no child shall be deemed to be physically or mentally abused for the sole reason that he is in good faith being furnished treatment by spiritual means through prayer alone, in accordance with the tenets and practices of a recognized church or religious denomination by a duly accredited practitioner thereof, or is not provided specified medical treatment in the practice of religious beliefs, or solely on the grounds of environmental factors that are beyond the control of the person responsible for the child's welfare, such as inadequate housing, furnishings, income, clothing, and medical care.

Serious Physical Injury—An injury caused by the acts or omissions of a perpetrator that does one of the following:
1. Causes the child severe pain.
2. Significantly impairs the child's physical functioning, either temporarily or permanently.
3. Is accompanied by physical evidence or a continuous pattern of separate, unexplained injuries to the child.

Serious Physical Neglect—A physical condition caused by the acts or missions of a perpetrator that endangers the child's life or development or impairs his functioning and is the result of one of the following:
1. Prolonged or repeated lack of supervision.
2. Failure to provide essentials of life, including adequate medical care.

Sexual Abuse—Any of the following when committed on a child by a perpetrator:
1. *Statutory Rape:* Sexual intercourse with a child who is less than 14 years of age by a person 18 years of age or older.
2. *Involuntary or Voluntary Deviate Sexual Intercourse:* Intercourse by mouth or rectum or with an animal.
3. *Sexual Assault:* Sexual involvement, including the touching or exposing of the sexual or other intimate parts of a person, for the purpose of arousing or gratifying sexual desire in either the perpetrator or the subject child.
4. *Incest:* Sexual intercourse with an ancestor or descendant—by blood or adoption—brother or sister of the whole or half blood, or an uncle, aunt, nephew or niece of the whole blood.
5. *Promoting Prostitution:* Inducing or encouraging a child to engage in prostitution.
6. *Rape:* Sexual intercourse by force or compulsion.
7. *Pornography:* Includes one of the following:
   a. The obscene photographing, filming, or depiction of children for commercial purposes.
   b. The obscene filming or photographing of children or showing of obscene films or photographs to arouse or gratify sexual desire in either the perpetrator, subject child, or viewing audience.

Serious Mental Injury—A psychological condition as diagnosed by a physician or licensed psychologist caused by the acts or omissions—including the refusal of appropriate treatment—of the perpetrator, which does one of the following:
1. Renders the child chronically and severely anxious, agitated, depressed, socially withdrawn, psychotic, or in reasonable fear that his life or safety is threatened.

2. Seriously interferes with the child's ability to accomplish age appropriate developmental and social tasks.

Neglect—The failure of a parent to provide for a child's physical, emotional, and moral needs, such as inadequate physical care, improper supervision, unlawfully keeping a child out of school, exposing a child to criminal or immoral influence. Includes:

- Unacceptable housekeeping standards

- Dangerous and inadequate housing

- Violence in the home

- Inadequate food or clothing

- Lack of medical care

- Improper supervision

- Poor moral atmosphere

- Failure to meet the child's educational needs

- Absence of basic parenting skills

NOTES

CHAPTER 2. The Vital Balance

1. Based on Abraham Maslow's "Hierarchy of Needs," *Toward a Psychology of Being* (New York: Van Nos Reinhold, 1955).
2. In *Cry Out!* (Nashville: Abingdon Press, 1984), when Peter was on the beach alone, trying to find a way to take care of himself, he came to this conclusion, which opened the door for God and others to help him (p. 169).
3. See *Cry Out!* pp. 20-21.
4. See *Renegade Saint* (Nashville: Abingdon Press, 1986), p. 54.

CHAPTER 5. The Damaging Effects of Abuse

1. John Bradshaw, *Healing the Shame That Binds You* (Deerfield Beach, Fla.: Health Communications, 1988), p. 11.
2. Sandra D. Wilson, *Released from Shame: Recovery for Adult Children of Dysfunctional Families* (Downers Grove, Ill.: Intervarsity Press, 1990), p. 41.
3. Steven Farmer, *Adult Children of Abusive Parents* (Los Angeles: Lowell House, 1989), p. 57.
4. Ibid., p. 74.

CHAPTER 8. Finding Relief for Symptoms

1. Michael J. Scott and Stephen G. Stradling, *Counseling for Post-Traumatic Stress Disorder* (Newbury Park, Calif.: Sage Publications, 1992), p. 10.
2. Ibid., p. 36.
3. Ibid., p. 43.